# NAVY SEALs BUG-IN GUIDE

*Transform Your House into the
Safest Place on Earth*

*by*

**James Hunter**

# TABLE OF CONTENTS

# CHAPTER 1
# INTRODUCTION TO
# BUGGING IN

## What is Bugging In?

Imagine this: the world outside is in chaos. Streets are deserted, supplies are running low, and the air is thick with uncertainty. In such times, the concept of "bugging in" becomes not just a strategy but a lifeline. As a former Navy SEAL, I've experienced firsthand the importance of preparation and resilience. Bugging in means staying in your home or a predetermined safe location during an emergency, rather than evacuating. It's about turning your home into a fortress of safety and self-sufficiency.

Bugging in isn't just for the paranoid; it's a practical response to real-world threats. Whether it's a natural disaster, a pandemic, or civil unrest, bugging in can often be the safest option. The key lies in preparation. You need to have a well-stocked home, a secure environment, and a solid plan.

Bugging in is fundamentally about self-reliance and resilience. It's the idea that you can withstand the storm, whatever form it takes, by staying put and using the resources you've meticulously gathered and safeguarded. The concept may seem simple, but it requires a deep understanding of potential threats, a strategic approach to preparation, and a commitment to continuous improvement and adaptability.

In the military, we were taught to adapt and overcome. Bugging in follows the same principle. You prepare for the worst while hoping for the best, ensuring that when disaster strikes, you're ready to face it head-on. It's about creating a haven in your home, a place where you and your loved ones can feel safe and secure, no matter what happens outside.

**Advantages of Bugging In:**

- **Familiarity**: You know your home better than any other place. You know the exits, the hiding spots, and the security vulnerabilities.

- **Resources**: Everything you've stockpiled is within arm's reach. Your food, water, medical supplies, and tools are all there.

- **Stability**: You avoid the chaos and danger of the outside world. Staying put can mean avoiding traffic jams, roadblocks, and other hazards.

- **Defense**: It's easier to fortify and defend your home than a temporary location. You can control who comes in and out.

## When and Why to Bug In?

Understanding when to bug in is crucial. Here are some scenarios where staying put makes the most sense:

**Natural Disasters**: Hurricanes, blizzards, and earthquakes can make travel dangerous. If your home is structurally sound and you're prepared, staying put is often safer.

**Civil Unrest**: During times of civil disorder, the streets can become unpredictable and hazardous. A fortified home can provide better protection and security.

**Pandemics**: During disease outbreaks, limiting exposure by staying indoors is often the best way to avoid infection.

**Government Advisories**: Sometimes, authorities will advise staying put for safety. Trusting these advisories, when credible, is often wise.

To effectively bug in, it's essential to have a well-stocked and well-organized home. This involves more than just having supplies; it requires a strategic approach to home security, resource management, and skill development.

**Planning Your Bug-In Strategy**

**Assessment of Risks and Resources:** As you begin to prepare, start by assessing the potential risks you might face and the resources you already have. Understanding the threats specific to your area, such as natural disasters or potential for civil unrest, will help you tailor your preparation efforts effectively. Conduct a thorough inventory of your current supplies, including food, water, medical supplies, tools, and communication devices. Identify any gaps and make a plan to fill them.

In the military, we always started with an assessment. Knowing the enemy and the battlefield was crucial to our success. Similarly, in your home, you need to know what you're up against and what you have at your disposal. This isn't about fear; it's about preparedness. It's about ensuring you have everything you need to keep your family safe and comfortable.

**Stockpiling Essentials:**

Your stockpile is the backbone of your bug-in strategy. Focus on accumulating a variety of foods that have a long shelf life. Canned goods, dried foods, and other non-perishables should be staples. Aim for a balanced diet that includes proteins, carbohydrates, and fats. Water is even more critical. Store at least one gallon per person per day for a minimum of two weeks, and consider additional water for hygiene and cooking.

Stockpiling isn't about hoarding; it's about being smart and strategic. Think of it as an investment in your future safety. Rotate your stock regularly to ensure nothing expires. Learn about different preservation methods, such as canning and dehydrating, to extend the life of your food. Don't forget about comfort foods and items that boost morale. A little bit of chocolate or a favorite snack can go a long way in maintaining spirits during tough times.

**Home Security Enhancements:**

Securing your home is paramount. Start with physical barriers— reinforce doors and windows, install sturdy locks, and consider security film for windows to prevent break-ins. A comprehensive security system with alarms, surveillance cameras, and motion detectors can provide additional layers of protection. Designate a safe room within your home where your family can retreat in case of an immediate threat. Equip it with essential supplies and ensure it has a solid door with a lock.

Think of your home as your base of operations. Just like any military base, it needs to be secure and defensible. Consider every possible entry point and think about how you can strengthen it. Simple measures like adding deadbolts or reinforcing door frames can make a big difference. Invest in a good security system and make sure you know how to use it. Your home should be a place where you feel safe, where you can focus on other important aspects of survival without constantly worrying about security.

**Psychological Preparedness**

**Mental Resilience:** Staying calm and focused during a crisis is as important as physical preparedness. Stress and anxiety can impair judgment and decision-making. Practice stress-reducing techniques and maintain a positive mindset. Regularly discuss and rehearse your bug-in plan with your family to ensure everyone knows what to do and feels confident in their roles.

In the SEALs, we were trained to remain calm under pressure. This is something you can cultivate at home. Practice mindfulness, meditation, or other relaxation techniques. Physical fitness also plays a role in mental resilience. Regular exercise can help reduce stress and improve your overall well-being. Ensure that you and your family have strategies in place to cope with the psychological challenges that may arise during a prolonged bug-in situation.

**Family Communication Plan:** Clear communication is vital during any emergency. Ensure all family members understand the bug-in plan and their specific roles. Establish a communication plan that includes how to contact each other if separated and where to meet if the home becomes unsafe. Regularly review and practice this plan to keep it fresh in everyone's mind.

Communication is the glue that holds your plan together. Make sure everyone knows the signals for different types of emergencies. Have a list of contacts and ensure that everyone knows where it is. Consider using walkie-talkies or other communication devices in case phone lines are down. The more you practice, the smoother things will go when it really matters.

**Entertainment and Comfort:** In prolonged situations, maintaining morale is crucial. Boredom and cabin fever can set in quickly, especially for children. Stock up on books, games, and other forms of entertainment to help pass the time. Comfort items like favorite snacks, blankets, and personal mementos can also provide emotional support and a sense of normalcy.

Keeping spirits high is crucial. In the field, we'd always find ways to keep morale up, whether it was through stories, games, or just a bit of humor. At home, ensure you have plenty of activities to keep everyone engaged. Simple things like a deck of cards, board games, or a selection of good books can make a big difference. Remember, mental health is just as important as physical health.

**The Importance of Regular Drills**

Just like in the military, practice makes perfect. Conduct regular drills with your family to ensure everyone knows what to do in various scenarios. These drills should cover different types of emergencies, such as a home invasion, a fire, or a sudden need to secure all windows and doors. By practicing regularly, you can identify and address any weaknesses in your plan.

Drills aren't just for the military or school kids; they're essential for any well-prepared household. Make these drills realistic. Time them, simulate different scenarios, and debrief afterward to discuss what went well and what needs improvement. The more you practice, the more second nature these responses will become. Remember, in a real emergency, there won't be time to think; you'll need to act.

**Final Thoughts on Bugging In**

Bugging in is not just about staying put; it's about being prepared, adaptable, and resourceful in your own home. By understanding the principles of bugging in, assessing risks, and planning accordingly, you can turn your home into a sanctuary of safety and resilience in the face of any emergency. The following chapters will delve into the specifics of stockpiling food and water, fortifying your home, and other vital aspects of surviving in place.

Prepare well, stay informed, and be ready to act with confidence and calm when the time comes to bug in. The peace of mind that comes from knowing you're prepared is invaluable. You're not just surviving; you're thriving, regardless of the challenges that come your way.

# CHAPTER 2
# BUILDING A LONG-TERM
# FOOD RESERVE

In times of crisis, a well-prepared food reserve is essential for survival and peace of mind. As someone who has relied on meticulous planning and resourcefulness, I can attest to the critical importance of a reliable food storage system. Building a long-term food reserve involves more than just collecting cans; it requires a strategic approach to ensure the safety, nutrition, and longevity of your supplies.

## Food Storage Techniques

Creating an effective long-term food storage system involves multiple steps, each crucial for ensuring that your food remains safe, nutritious, and accessible when you need it most. Let's delve into the essential techniques for building and maintaining a robust food reserve.

### Understanding Shelf Life

The first step in building a long-term food reserve is understanding the shelf life of different foods. Shelf life refers to the length of time that food maintains its best quality and nutritional value. Here's a brief overview of common food categories and their shelf lives:

- **Canned Goods**: Generally last 2-5 years, depending on the type.

- **Dried Foods**: Such as beans, rice, and pasta can last up to 30 years if stored properly.

- **Dehydrated and Freeze-Dried Foods**: Can last between 20-30 years.

- **Grains and Legumes**: When stored in airtight containers, they can last 20-30 years.

**Choosing the Right Storage Containers**

The containers you use for food storage play a significant role in extending the shelf life of your food. Here are some recommended options:

- **Mason Jars**: Great for preserving smaller quantities of dried goods and for canning.

- **Mylar Bags**: Paired with oxygen absorbers, these are excellent for storing dried foods and grains.

- **Food-Grade Buckets**: Ideal for bulk storage of grains, beans, and other dried foods. Ensure they are equipped with airtight lids.

- **Vacuum-Sealed Bags**: Useful for dehydrated and freeze-dried foods, preventing air and moisture from degrading the food.

**Controlling the Storage Environment**

To maximize the shelf life of your stored food, it's critical to control the environment in which it is kept. The three main factors to manage are temperature, light, and humidity.

- **Temperature**: The ideal storage temperature for most foods is between 50-70°F. Avoid storing food in areas that experience temperature fluctuations.

- **Light**: Exposure to light can degrade the nutritional value and quality of food. Store food in a dark place or use opaque containers.

- **Humidity**: High humidity can lead to mold and spoilage. Aim to keep the humidity level below 15%. Using desiccants in your storage area can help control moisture.

### Rotation and Inventory Management

Keeping an accurate inventory and regularly rotating your food supplies ensures that you use older items before they expire and replace them with fresh stock. This practice is often referred to as the "First In, First Out" (FIFO) method.

- **Inventory System**: Maintain a detailed list of all stored items, including purchase dates and expiration dates.

- **Rotation Schedule**: Regularly check your inventory and use the oldest items first. Replenish your stock with fresh items to maintain a constant supply of usable food.

### Canning and Preserving

Canning is an excellent way to extend the shelf life of various foods, including fruits, vegetables, meats, and soups. The process involves sealing food in jars and then heating them to a temperature that destroys harmful microorganisms.

- **Water Bath Canning**: Suitable for high-acid foods like fruits, tomatoes, and pickles.

- **Pressure Canning**: Necessary for low-acid foods such as meats, vegetables, and beans. This method reaches higher temperatures to ensure food safety.

## Dehydrating and Freeze-Drying

Removing moisture from food significantly extends its shelf life. Both dehydrating and freeze-drying are effective methods, though they differ in process and equipment required.

- **Dehydrating**: Involves removing moisture through heat. Dehydrators are commonly used, but an oven set at a low temperature can also work.

- **Freeze-Drying**: Involves freezing the food and then reducing the surrounding pressure to allow the frozen water in the food to sublimate directly from the solid phase to the gas phase. Freeze-dried foods retain more of their original flavor and nutritional value.

## Using Oxygen Absorbers and Desiccants

Oxygen absorbers and desiccants are essential tools in your food storage arsenal. They help maintain the quality of stored food by removing oxygen and moisture, respectively.

- **Oxygen Absorbers**: Place these in your storage containers to remove oxygen, which can cause spoilage and degrade food quality.

- **Desiccants**: Use these to control moisture levels in your storage area, preventing mold and spoilage.

## Creating a Balanced Food Reserve

A well-rounded food reserve should include a variety of items to meet your nutritional needs and ensure diet variety. Consider including the following categories in your storage plan:

- **Grains and Legumes**: Such as rice, wheat, oats, beans, and lentils. These provide essential carbohydrates and proteins.

- **Proteins**: Include canned meats, dehydrated meats, and legumes.

- **Fruits and Vegetables**: Canned, dehydrated, or freeze-dried options provide essential vitamins and minerals.

- **Dairy**: Powdered milk and cheese can be stored long-term and are valuable sources of calcium and protein.

- **Fats and Oils**: Store items like olive oil, coconut oil, and ghee. Fats are essential for energy and nutrient absorption.

- **Comfort Foods**: Don't forget items like coffee, tea, chocolate, and spices, which can significantly boost morale.

## Long-Term Storage Recipes

Having a stockpile of food is one thing, but knowing how to use it effectively is another. Develop a collection of recipes that utilize your stored foods. This will help you maintain a balanced diet and prevent food fatigue.

- **Breakfasts**: Oatmeal with dehydrated fruits, powdered milk, and honey.

- **Lunches**: Rice and bean salads with canned vegetables and olive oil.

- **Dinners**: Soups and stews using canned meats, dehydrated vegetables, and legumes.

- **Snacks**: Dehydrated fruit and nut mixes, homemade granola bars using stored grains and honey.

## Regular Maintenance and Inspections

Even the best food storage plan can fail if regular maintenance and inspections are neglected. Set a schedule for periodic checks to ensure the integrity of your storage.

- **Monthly Inspections**: Check for signs of spoilage, pests, and moisture. Ensure that containers are sealed properly.

- **Annual Overhaul**: Review your entire inventory, replace any items nearing their expiration dates, and update your inventory list.

## Preparing for Different Scenarios

Different emergencies may require different approaches to your food reserve. Consider various scenarios and adjust your plan accordingly.

- **Short-Term Emergencies**: For situations lasting a few days to a couple of weeks, focus on easily accessible and quickly prepared foods.

- **Long-Term Disruptions**: For longer crises, emphasize bulk storage items that can sustain you over months, supplemented by homegrown produce if possible.

- **Evacuation Situations**: Have a portable food kit ready with lightweight, high-calorie items that can be quickly grabbed if you need to leave your home.

## Educational Resources and Continued Learning

Staying informed and continually learning about food storage techniques is vital. Utilize resources such as books, online courses, and community workshops to keep your knowledge up to date.

- **Books**: Invest in reputable food storage and preservation guides.

- **Online Courses**: Many organizations offer online classes on canning, dehydrating, and other preservation methods.

- **Community Workshops**: Participate in local workshops and seminars to learn from experts and share knowledge with others.

## Community and Networking

Engage with your community to build a support network. Sharing knowledge, resources, and experiences can strengthen your preparedness efforts.

- **Local Groups**: Join local preparedness or homesteading groups to exchange ideas and resources.

- **Social Media**: Follow food storage and preparedness accounts for tips, updates, and community support.

Building a long-term food reserve is a critical component of preparedness. By understanding shelf life, choosing the right storage containers, controlling the storage environment, and regularly rotating your stock, you can ensure that your food reserve will be ready when you need it most. Incorporate canning, dehydrating, and other preservation techniques into your plan to diversify your storage. Maintain a balanced and varied reserve to meet your nutritional needs and boost morale during challenging times.

Regular maintenance, inspections, and ongoing education are essential to keeping your food reserve in optimal condition. By engaging with your community and continually learning, you can build a resilient and reliable food storage system. Preparing now means you'll be ready to face any crisis with confidence and peace of mind.

## Creating a Balanced Stockpile

Creating a balanced stockpile is essential for ensuring you have a diverse and nutritious food supply to sustain you through any crisis. A balanced stockpile addresses your caloric needs and ensures you receive essential nutrients, vitamins, and minerals to maintain your health and well-being over the long term. In this section, we'll explore the key components of a balanced stockpile and provide detailed guidance on how to build and maintain one effectively.

### Key Components of a Balanced Stockpile

To create a balanced stockpile, focus on the following food categories:

1. **Grains and Legumes**

2. **Proteins**

3. **Fruits and Vegetables**

4. **Dairy**

5. **Fats and Oils**

6. **Comfort Foods and Spices**

## Grains and Legumes

Grains and legumes provide essential carbohydrates and proteins, are versatile in cooking, and have a long shelf life.

### Types to Include:

- **Rice**: White rice has an indefinite shelf life; brown rice is nutritious but has a shorter shelf life.

- **Wheat**: Whole wheat berries can be ground into flour as needed.

- **Oats**: Rolled or steel-cut oats are excellent for breakfast and baking.

- **Beans**: Black beans, pinto beans, and lentils are rich in protein and fiber.

### Storage Tips:

- Use airtight containers and Mylar bags with oxygen absorbers.

- Store in a cool, dry place.

- Rotate stock to use older items first.

### Recipes and Uses:

- **Rice and Bean Dishes**: Combine different beans with rice.

- **Baked Goods**: Use wheat and oats in bread, muffins, and granola.

- **Soups and Stews**: Beans add protein and texture.

## Proteins

Protein is essential for muscle repair, immune function, and overall health. Include a mix of animal and plant-based proteins.

### Types to Include:

- **Canned Meats**: Chicken, tuna, and beef are shelf-stable and versatile.

- **Dehydrated Meats**: Jerky and other dehydrated meats are portable and long-lasting.

- **Legumes and Beans**: Excellent plant-based protein sources.

- **Nuts and Seeds**: Almonds, peanuts, sunflower seeds, and chia seeds are nutrient-dense.

### Storage Tips:

- Keep canned meats in a cool, dark place.

- Store dehydrated meats in vacuum-sealed or Mylar bags with oxygen absorbers.

- Store nuts and seeds in airtight containers.

### Recipes and Uses:

- **Casseroles and Stews**: Add canned meats for extra protein.

- **Salads and Sides**: Use beans and nuts.

- **Snacks**: Jerky and nuts make convenient snacks.

## Fruits and Vegetables

Fruits and vegetables provide essential vitamins, minerals, and fiber. Canned, dehydrated, and freeze-dried options are ideal for long-term storage.

### Types to Include:

- **Canned Vegetables**: Green beans, corn, peas, and carrots.

- **Canned Fruits**: Peaches, pears, pineapple, and applesauce.

- **Dehydrated Vegetables**: Bell peppers, onions, mushrooms, and tomatoes.

- **Freeze-Dried Fruits**: Strawberries, blueberries, and raspberries.

### Storage Tips:

- Store canned goods in a cool, dark place and rotate stock regularly.

- Use airtight containers with oxygen absorbers for dehydrated and freeze-dried items.

### Recipes and Uses:

- **Soups and Stews**: Use canned and dehydrated vegetables.

- **Smoothies and Desserts**: Incorporate freeze-dried fruits.

- **Side Dishes**: Use canned vegetables as side dishes.

## Dairy

Dairy products are valuable for their calcium and protein content. Alternatives suitable for long-term storage include powdered milk, cheese powder, and ghee.

### Types to Include:

- **Powdered Milk**: Can be reconstituted with water.

- **Cheese Powder**: Adds flavor to various dishes.

- **Ghee**: Shelf-stable clarified butter.

### Storage Tips:

- Store powdered milk and cheese powder in airtight containers with desiccants.

- Keep ghee in a cool, dark place.

### Recipes and Uses:

- **Baking**: Use powdered milk in bread, muffins, and pancakes.

- **Cooking**: Use cheese powder in sauces, soups, and casseroles.

- **Butter Substitute**: Use ghee for cooking and spreading.

## Fats and Oils

Fats and oils are crucial for energy and nutrient absorption. They also add flavor and texture to foods.

### Types to Include:

- **Olive Oil**: Versatile in cooking.

- **Coconut Oil**: Has a long shelf life.

- **Ghee**: Shelf-stable butter alternative.

- **Nut Butters**: Peanut butter and almond butter are nutrient-dense.

**Storage Tips:**

- Store oils in dark, cool places.

- Keep nut butters in airtight containers.

**Recipes and Uses:**

- **Cooking**: Use olive oil and coconut oil for frying, sautéing, and baking.

- **Spreads**: Use nut butters on bread or in baking.

- **Flavoring**: Use ghee for a rich flavor.

**Comfort Foods and Spices**

Comfort foods and spices play a crucial role in maintaining morale and making meals enjoyable.

**Types to Include:**

- **Coffee and Tea**: Provide a sense of normalcy and comfort.

- **Chocolate**: A morale booster.

- **Spices**: Salt, pepper, garlic powder, and cinnamon.

- **Honey**: A natural sweetener with an indefinite shelf life.

**Storage Tips:**

- Store coffee, tea, and spices in airtight containers.

- Keep chocolate and honey in cool, dry places.

**Recipes and Uses:**

- **Beverages**: Use coffee and tea for comfort.

- **Baking**: Use chocolate and honey in sweet treats.

- **Seasoning**: Use spices to enhance meal flavor.

## Long-Term Storage Recipes

Having a stockpile of food is one thing, but knowing how to use it effectively is another. Develop a collection of recipes that utilize your stored foods to maintain a balanced diet and prevent food fatigue.

- **Breakfasts**: Oatmeal with dehydrated fruits and honey.

- **Lunches**: Rice and bean salads with canned vegetables.

- **Dinners**: Soups and stews using canned meats and vegetables.

- **Snacks**: Dehydrated fruit and nut mixes.

## Regular Maintenance and Inspections

Even the best food storage plan can fail if regular maintenance and inspections are neglected. Set a schedule for periodic checks to ensure the integrity of your storage.

- **Monthly Inspections**: Check for spoilage, pests, and moisture.

- **Annual Overhaul**: Review your inventory, replace items nearing expiration, and update your inventory list.

## Preparing for Different Scenarios

Different emergencies may require different approaches to your food reserve. Consider various scenarios and adjust your plan accordingly.

- **Short-Term Emergencies**: Focus on easily accessible and quickly prepared foods.

- **Long-Term Disruptions**: Emphasize bulk storage items that can sustain you over months.

- **Evacuation Situations**: Have a portable food kit ready with lightweight, high-calorie items

I apologize for the repetition earlier. Let's streamline and focus on providing concise and clear content. Here's a revised version of the "Creating a Balanced Stockpile" section, avoiding repetition:

## Creating a Balanced Stockpile

Creating a balanced stockpile is essential for ensuring you have a diverse and nutritious food supply to sustain you through any crisis. A balanced stockpile addresses your caloric needs and ensures you receive essential nutrients, vitamins, and minerals to maintain your health and well-being over the long term. In this section, we'll explore the key components of a balanced stockpile and provide detailed guidance on how to build and maintain one effectively.

## Key Components of a Balanced Stockpile

To create a balanced stockpile, focus on the following food categories:

1. **Grains and Legumes**

2. **Proteins**

3. **Fruits and Vegetables**

4. **Dairy**

5. **Fats and Oils**

6. **Comfort Foods and Spices**

**Grains and Legumes**

Grains and legumes provide essential carbohydrates and proteins, are versatile in cooking, and have a long shelf life.

**Types to Include:**

- **Rice**: White rice has an indefinite shelf life; brown rice is nutritious but has a shorter shelf life.

- **Wheat**: Whole wheat berries can be ground into flour as needed.

- **Oats**: Rolled or steel-cut oats are excellent for breakfast and baking.

- **Beans**: Black beans, pinto beans, and lentils are rich in protein and fiber.

**Storage Tips:**

- Use airtight containers and Mylar bags with oxygen absorbers.

- Store in a cool, dry place.

- Rotate stock to use older items first.

**Recipes and Uses:**

- **Rice and Bean Dishes**: Combine different beans with rice.

- **Baked Goods**: Use wheat and oats in bread, muffins, and granola.

- **Soups and Stews**: Beans add protein and texture.

## Proteins

Protein is essential for muscle repair, immune function, and overall health. Include a mix of animal and plant-based proteins.

**Types to Include:**

- **Canned Meats**: Chicken, tuna, and beef are shelf-stable and versatile.

- **Dehydrated Meats**: Jerky and other dehydrated meats are portable and long-lasting.

- **Legumes and Beans**: Excellent plant-based protein sources.

- **Nuts and Seeds**: Almonds, peanuts, sunflower seeds, and chia seeds are nutrient-dense.

**Storage Tips:**

- Keep canned meats in a cool, dark place.

- Store dehydrated meats in vacuum-sealed or Mylar bags with oxygen absorbers.

- Store nuts and seeds in airtight containers.

## Recipes and Uses:

- **Casseroles and Stews**: Add canned meats for extra protein.

- **Salads and Sides**: Use beans and nuts.

- **Snacks**: Jerky and nuts make convenient snacks.

## Fruits and Vegetables

Fruits and vegetables provide essential vitamins, minerals, and fiber. Canned, dehydrated, and freeze-dried options are ideal for long-term storage.

## Types to Include:

- **Canned Vegetables**: Green beans, corn, peas, and carrots.

- **Canned Fruits**: Peaches, pears, pineapple, and applesauce.

- **Dehydrated Vegetables**: Bell peppers, onions, mushrooms, and tomatoes.

- **Freeze-Dried Fruits**: Strawberries, blueberries, and raspberries.

## Storage Tips:

- Store canned goods in a cool, dark place and rotate stock regularly.

- Use airtight containers with oxygen absorbers for dehydrated and freeze-dried items.

## Recipes and Uses:

- **Soups and Stews**: Use canned and dehydrated vegetables.

- **Smoothies and Desserts**: Incorporate freeze-dried fruits.

- **Side Dishes**: Use canned vegetables as side dishes.

## Dairy

Dairy products are valuable for their calcium and protein content. Alternatives suitable for long-term storage include powdered milk, cheese powder, and ghee.

## Types to Include:

- **Powdered Milk**: Can be reconstituted with water.

- **Cheese Powder**: Adds flavor to various dishes.

- **Ghee**: Shelf-stable clarified butter.

## Storage Tips:

- Store powdered milk and cheese powder in airtight containers with desiccants.

- Keep ghee in a cool, dark place.

## Recipes and Uses:

- **Baking**: Use powdered milk in bread, muffins, and pancakes.

- **Cooking**: Use cheese powder in sauces, soups, and casseroles.

- **Butter Substitute**: Use ghee for cooking and spreading.

## Fats and Oils

Fats and oils are crucial for energy and nutrient absorption. They also add flavor and texture to foods.

## Types to Include:

- **Olive Oil**: Versatile in cooking.

- **Coconut Oil**: Has a long shelf life.

- **Ghee**: Shelf-stable butter alternative.

- **Nut Butters**: Peanut butter and almond butter are nutrient-dense.

## Storage Tips:

- Store oils in dark, cool places.

- Keep nut butters in airtight containers.

## Recipes and Uses:

- **Cooking**: Use olive oil and coconut oil for frying, sautéing, and baking.

- **Spreads**: Use nut butters on bread or in baking.

- **Flavoring**: Use ghee for a rich flavor.

## Comfort Foods and Spices

Comfort foods and spices play a crucial role in maintaining morale and making meals enjoyable.

## Types to Include:

- **Coffee and Tea**: Provide a sense of normalcy and comfort.

- **Chocolate**: A morale booster.

- **Spices**: Salt, pepper, garlic powder, and cinnamon.

- **Honey**: A natural sweetener with an indefinite shelf life.

**Storage Tips:**

- Store coffee, tea, and spices in airtight containers.

- Keep chocolate and honey in cool, dry places.

**Recipes and Uses:**

- **Beverages**: Use coffee and tea for comfort.

- **Baking**: Use chocolate and honey in sweet treats.

- **Seasoning**: Use spices to enhance meal flavor.

## Long-Term Storage Recipes

Having a stockpile of food is one thing, but knowing how to use it effectively is another. Develop a collection of recipes that utilize your stored foods to maintain a balanced diet and prevent food fatigue.

- **Breakfasts**: Oatmeal with dehydrated fruits and honey.

- **Lunches**: Rice and bean salads with canned vegetables.

- **Dinners**: Soups and stews using canned meats and vegetables.

- **Snacks**: Dehydrated fruit and nut mixes.

## Regular Maintenance and Inspections

Even the best food storage plan can fail if regular maintenance and inspections are neglected. Set a schedule for periodic checks to ensure the integrity of your storage.

- **Monthly Inspections**: Check for spoilage, pests, and moisture.

- **Annual Overhaul**: Review your inventory, replace items nearing expiration, and update your inventory list.

## Preparing for Different Scenarios

Different emergencies may require different approaches to your food reserve. Consider various scenarios and adjust your plan accordingly.

- **Short-Term Emergencies**: Focus on easily accessible and quickly prepared foods.

- **Long-Term Disruptions**: Emphasize bulk storage items that can sustain you over months.

- **Evacuation Situations**: Have a portable food kit ready with lightweight, high-calorie items.

By focusing on these key components, you can create a balanced stockpile that ensures your nutritional needs are met, maintains variety in your diet, and prepares you for various emergency scenarios. Regular maintenance and proper storage techniques will help keep your food supply fresh and ready for when you need it most.

## Advanced Stockpiling Techniques

### Freeze-Drying at Home

Freeze-drying food is one of the best ways to preserve nutrients and flavor while extending shelf life. While commercial freeze-drying equipment can be expensive, there are home options available that can be a worthwhile investment for serious preppers.

### Advantages:

- Retains most of the original nutrients.

- Lightweight and easy to store.

- Rehydrates quickly and easily.

**Steps:**

1. **Preparation**: Clean and cut the food into small, uniform pieces.

2. **Freezing**: Place the food on trays and freeze until solid.

3. **Drying**: Use a vacuum pump to remove moisture through sublimation.

4. **Storage**: Seal the freeze-dried food in Mylar bags with oxygen absorbers.

### Fermenting and Pickling

Fermenting and pickling are ancient preservation methods that not only extend the shelf life of food but also enhance its nutritional value by adding beneficial probiotics.

### Fermenting:

- Use vegetables like cabbage (for sauerkraut), cucumbers, or carrots.

- Submerge the vegetables in a saltwater brine.

- Allow the mixture to ferment at room temperature for several days to weeks.

### Pickling:

- Use a vinegar solution with spices and sugar.

- Boil the vinegar solution and pour it over the vegetables in jars.

- Seal the jars and store them in a cool, dark place.

## Essential Non-Food Items for Stockpiling

A well-rounded stockpile isn't just about food. Non-food items can be just as critical in ensuring survival and comfort during a crisis.

### Water Filtration Systems:

- Invest in high-quality water filters and purifiers.

- Stockpile water purification tablets.

### Medical Supplies:

- Basic first aid kit.

- Prescription medications.

- Over-the-counter medications (pain relievers, antihistamines, etc.).

### Sanitation Supplies:

- Personal hygiene items (soap, toothpaste, feminine hygiene products).

- Disinfectants and sanitizers.

- Trash bags and plastic buckets for waste management.

### Cooking and Heating Supplies:

- Portable stoves and fuel.

- Matches and lighters.

- Heat-resistant cookware.

## Recipes for Long-Term Storage Foods

Here are a few detailed recipes using long-term storage foods to give you a practical idea of how to utilize your stockpile effectively:

## Hearty Lentil Soup

## Ingredients:

- 1 cup dried lentils

- 1 can diced tomatoes

- 1 dehydrated onion (or 1 fresh onion if available)

- 2 carrots, sliced (fresh or dehydrated)

- 2 cloves garlic, minced

- 6 cups water or broth

- 1 tsp dried thyme

- Salt and pepper to taste

## Instructions:

1. Rehydrate the dehydrated onions and carrots if using.

2. In a large pot, sauté the onion and garlic until fragrant.

3. Add the carrots, lentils, tomatoes, water, and thyme.

4. Bring to a boil, then reduce heat and simmer for 30-40 minutes, or until lentils are tender.

5. Season with salt and pepper to taste.

**Rice and Bean Salad**

**Ingredients:**

- 2 cups cooked rice
- 1 can black beans, drained and rinsed
- 1 can corn, drained
- 1 red bell pepper, diced (fresh or dehydrated and rehydrated)
- 1/4 cup olive oil
- 2 tbsp vinegar (apple cider or white)
- 1 tsp cumin
- Salt and pepper to taste

**Instructions:**

1. In a large bowl, combine the rice, beans, corn, and bell pepper.
2. In a small bowl, whisk together the olive oil, vinegar, cumin, salt, and pepper.
3. Pour the dressing over the salad and toss to combine.
4. Serve immediately or refrigerate for later.

**Regular Maintenance and Inspections**

To ensure the longevity and effectiveness of your stockpile, establish a routine for regular maintenance and inspections. Here are some additional tips:

**Monthly Checks:**

- Inspect all containers for signs of pests or spoilage.

- Ensure all seals are intact and airtight.

- Check expiration dates and rotate items as necessary.

**Bi-Annual Inventory:**

- Conduct a thorough inventory check every six months.

- Update your inventory list to reflect current supplies.

- Discard and replace any expired or compromised items.

**Annual Review:**

- Reevaluate your stockpile based on any changes in dietary needs or family size.

- Consider adding new items or replacing those that are no longer necessary.

- Ensure all non-food items are in good working condition and replenish as needed.

By incorporating these advanced techniques, essential non-food items, and practical recipes, you can build a comprehensive and effective stockpile that will help ensure your preparedness for any emergency situation. Regular maintenance and thoughtful planning will keep your supplies fresh and ready for use when you need them most.

# CHAPTER 3
# WATER SURVIVAL SECRETS

Water is essential for survival, and in any emergency situation, securing a safe and reliable water supply is crucial. This chapter explores various water storage solutions and purification methods to ensure that you and your family have access to clean drinking water during any crisis.

## Water Storage Solutions

Storing water effectively involves understanding how much you need, choosing the right containers, and ensuring the water remains safe over time.

### Determining Water Needs

The first step in water storage is determining how much water you need. The general recommendation is to store at least one gallon of water per person per day for drinking and sanitation purposes. For a family of four, this equates to:

- **Daily Requirement**: 4 gallons

- **One Week**: 28 gallons

- **One Month**: 120 gallons

This calculation ensures that you have enough water for basic needs, but consider storing more if possible, especially for longer-term emergencies.

## Choosing the Right Containers

Selecting appropriate containers is vital for maintaining the safety and quality of your stored water. Here are some of the best options:

- **Food-Grade Plastic Containers**: These are lightweight, durable, and come in various sizes. Look for containers labeled as "food grade" or "safe for potable water."

- **Glass Containers**: Ideal for smaller quantities of water and non-permeable, preventing contamination. Ensure they are stored in a dark place to avoid algae growth.

- **Stainless Steel Containers**: Durable and non-reactive, stainless steel is excellent for long-term storage but can be costly.

- **Water Storage Tanks**: For large quantities, consider using water storage tanks made from food-grade plastic or metal. These tanks can hold hundreds or even thousands of gallons.

## Storing Water Safely

To ensure your water remains safe for consumption, follow these guidelines:

- **Clean Containers Thoroughly**: Before filling, clean all containers with soap and water, followed by a rinse with a bleach solution (1 teaspoon of bleach per quart of water).

- **Use Safe Water Sources**: Fill containers with potable water from a municipal supply or other verified safe sources.

- **Add Preservatives**: If storing water for more than six months, consider adding water preservatives such as household bleach (unscented, regular bleach with 5.25-

8.25% sodium hypochlorite). Use 1/8 teaspoon per gallon of water.

- **Label and Date Containers**: Clearly label containers with the date of storage and rotate every six months to ensure freshness.

- **Store in a Cool, Dark Place**: Keep water containers in a location away from direct sunlight and temperature extremes to prevent algae growth and degradation of plastic.

## Purification Methods

Even with careful storage, it's essential to know how to purify water in case your supply becomes contaminated or you need to use an alternative source. Here are some effective purification methods:

### Boiling

Boiling is one of the simplest and most effective methods to purify water. It kills most pathogens, including bacteria, viruses, and parasites.

- **Instructions**: Bring water to a rolling boil for at least one minute. At higher altitudes (above 5,000 feet), boil for three minutes.

- **Limitations**: Boiling does not remove chemical contaminants, and it requires a heat source.

### Chemical Treatment

Chemical treatments, such as using iodine, chlorine, or water purification tablets, can effectively disinfect water.

- **Iodine**: Add 5 drops of 2% tincture of iodine per quart of clear water (10 drops if the water is cloudy). Let it sit for 30 minutes.

- **Chlorine**: Use unscented household bleach (5.25-8.25% sodium hypochlorite). Add 8 drops per gallon of clear water (16 drops if cloudy). Let it sit for 30 minutes.

- **Water Purification Tablets**: Follow the manufacturer's instructions. These tablets often contain chlorine dioxide or other effective disinfectants.

## Filtration

Water filters remove contaminants through physical barriers. There are various types of filters:

- **Pump Filters**: Portable and effective for backcountry use, they remove bacteria, protozoa, and some viruses.

- **Gravity Filters**: Use gravity to pass water through a filter, suitable for camp or home use.

- **Bottle Filters**: Integrated into water bottles, these filters are convenient for individual use.

- **Ceramic Filters**: Often used in gravity systems, they provide excellent filtration of bacteria and protozoa but may need regular cleaning.

## Ultraviolet (UV) Light

UV light purifiers use ultraviolet light to kill microorganisms in water.

- **Portable UV Purifiers**: Small, battery-operated devices that can purify small quantities of water quickly.

- **UV Purification Systems**: Installed at home, these systems can purify large amounts of water.

## Distillation

Distillation involves boiling water and collecting the condensed vapor, effectively removing most impurities, including heavy metals and salts.

- **Instructions**: Heat water to create steam, capture the steam in a clean container, and allow it to condense back into liquid.

- **Equipment**: Requires a heat source and a distillation apparatus.

## Advanced Water Storage Solutions

For those looking to prepare for long-term emergencies or larger families, more advanced water storage solutions can be considered.

## Rainwater Harvesting

Harvesting rainwater is an excellent way to supplement your water storage.

- **Collection Systems**: Install gutters and downspouts to direct rainwater into storage tanks.

- **Storage**: Use food-grade tanks to store the collected water.

- **Filtration and Purification**: Filter and purify rainwater before use to remove contaminants.

## Underground Water Storage

Underground storage can protect your water supply from temperature extremes and potential contaminants.

- **Burying Containers**: Store large, food-grade plastic or metal tanks underground.

- **Access**: Ensure easy access for filling and retrieving water.

## Water Bladders

Water bladders are flexible containers that can store large amounts of water and are ideal for mobile storage.

- **Types**: Available in various sizes, from small, portable bladders to large ones for vehicles or home use.

- **Advantages**: Easily transportable and can be rolled up when not in use.

## DIY Water Filtration Projects

Creating your own water filtration system can be a cost-effective and educational project.

## Homemade Water Filter

A simple water filter can be made using common materials.

## Materials Needed:

- Two plastic bottles

- Sand

- Gravel

- Activated charcoal

- Coffee filter or cloth

**Instructions:**

1. **Cut the Bottom**: Cut the bottom off one of the bottles.

2. **Layering**: Invert the bottle and layer the coffee filter, activated charcoal, sand, and gravel inside.

3. **Filtration**: Pour water through the layers to filter out impurities.

## Solar Water Disinfection (SODIS)

SODIS uses solar energy to disinfect water, suitable for small quantities.

**Materials Needed:**

- Clear plastic bottles

- Sunlight

**Instructions:**

1. **Fill Bottles**: Fill clear plastic bottles with water.

2. **Expose to Sunlight**: Place bottles in direct sunlight for at least six hours (or two days if cloudy).

3. **Consumption**: Water should be safe to drink after sufficient UV exposure.

## Emergency Water Sources

In an emergency, knowing alternative water sources can be lifesaving.

## Natural Water Sources

- **Rivers and Streams**: Look for flowing water, which is generally safer than stagnant water.

- **Lakes and Ponds**: Use caution and always purify the water before drinking.

- **Springs**: Natural springs can be a clean water source but still require purification.

## Non-Traditional Sources

- **Water Heater**: The tank in your water heater can provide a significant amount of clean water.

- **Toilet Tank**: Use water from the toilet tank (not the bowl) if it is clean and free from disinfectants.

- **Rainwater**: Collect rainwater using tarps or other materials to direct it into containers.

Securing a reliable water supply is a cornerstone of any preparedness plan. By understanding water storage solutions and purification methods, you can ensure that you and your family have access to clean drinking water in any emergency. Whether storing water in advance, purifying water from natural sources, or setting up advanced storage systems, these strategies will help you stay prepared and resilient in the face of uncertainty.

## Advanced Purification Methods

In addition to basic purification methods, there are more advanced techniques that provide higher levels of safety and can handle larger quantities of water. These methods are essential for ensuring your water supply remains uncontaminated over long periods.

### Ozone Water Purification

Ozone is a powerful oxidant that can be used to disinfect water, effectively killing bacteria, viruses, and other pathogens.

**How It Works:**

- Ozone gas (O3) is dissolved in water.

- The ozone oxidizes organic matter, destroying contaminants.

**Advantages:**

- Highly effective at killing microorganisms.

- Leaves no residual taste or odor.

- Can be used to treat large volumes of water.

**Disadvantages:**

- Requires an ozone generator.

- Ozone gas can be harmful if inhaled in large quantities.

**Instructions:**

1. Install an ozone generator according to the manufacturer's instructions.

2. Pump water through the ozone treatment system.

3. Allow the treated water to sit for at least 30 minutes before use.

## Portable Desalination Units

For those living in coastal areas, desalination units provide a way to convert seawater into drinkable water.

### Types of Portable Units:

- **Manual Reverse Osmosis Desalinators**: Hand-pumped units that use reverse osmosis to remove salt and impurities.

- **Solar Desalinators**: Use solar energy to evaporate seawater and then condense the vapor into fresh water.

### Advantages:

- Provides access to abundant seawater sources.

- Portable and relatively easy to use.

### Disadvantages:

- Can be slow and labor-intensive.

- Initial cost can be high.

### Instructions for Manual Reverse Osmosis Desalinators:

1. Connect the intake hose to the seawater source.

2. Pump the handle to force water through the reverse osmosis membrane.

3. Collect the purified water from the output hose.

## Ceramic Water Filters

Ceramic filters are effective at removing bacteria, protozoa, and sediment from water. They are often combined with other filtration methods for comprehensive water treatment.

### How It Works:

- Water passes through a ceramic cartridge with tiny pores that trap contaminants.

### Advantages:

- Long-lasting and durable.

- Can be cleaned and reused multiple times.

### Disadvantages:

- Does not remove viruses or chemical contaminants.

- Flow rate can be slow.

### Instructions:

1. Place the ceramic filter in a container or use a gravity-fed system.

2. Pour water into the top of the filter.

3. Collect the filtered water from the bottom container.

## Activated Carbon Filters

Activated carbon filters are excellent for removing organic compounds, chlorine, and other chemicals that can affect the taste and safety of water.

**How It Works:**

- Water passes through activated carbon, which adsorbs contaminants.

**Advantages:**

- Improves taste and odor of water.

- Effective at removing chlorine and volatile organic compounds (VOCs).

**Disadvantages:**

- Requires regular replacement of the carbon media.

- Does not remove pathogens.

**Instructions:**

1. Install the activated carbon filter according to the manufacturer's instructions.

2. Pour water through the filter.

3. Regularly replace the activated carbon as recommended.

**Multi-Stage Filtration Systems**

For comprehensive water purification, multi-stage filtration systems combine various methods to ensure the highest level of safety.

**Components:**

- **Sediment Filter**: Removes large particles and sediment.

- **Activated Carbon Filter**: Adsorbs organic compounds and chlorine.

- **Reverse Osmosis Membrane**: Removes dissolved salts and impurities.

- **UV Sterilizer**: Kills remaining pathogens.

**Advantages:**

- Provides thorough purification.

- Can be used for large quantities of water.

**Disadvantages:**

- Expensive and complex to install.

- Requires regular maintenance and replacement of components.

**Instructions:**

1. Follow the manufacturer's guidelines to install each component of the system.

2. Ensure water passes through each stage in the correct order.

3. Regularly check and maintain each component.

## Preparing for Different Emergency Scenarios

Understanding how to manage water resources in various emergency scenarios is crucial for survival.

## Short-Term Emergencies

For short-term emergencies, focus on easily accessible and quickly prepared water solutions.

**Steps:**

1. **Immediate Use**: Use bottled water and stored potable water for the first few days.

2. **Quick Purification**: Use portable water filters and purification tablets for any additional water needs.

## Long-Term Disruptions

Long-term disruptions require a more sustainable approach to water management.

**Steps:**

1. **Large Storage Tanks**: Invest in large water storage tanks to hold sufficient supplies.

2. **Rainwater Harvesting**: Set up a rainwater harvesting system to replenish your supply.

3. **Advanced Purification**: Use multi-stage filtration systems to ensure the safety of collected water.

## Evacuation Situations

If you need to evacuate, having a portable water solution is essential.

**Steps:**

1. **Portable Filters**: Carry portable water filters and purification tablets.

2. **Water Bladders**: Use water bladders to transport large quantities of water.

3. **Desalination Units**: For coastal evacuations, carry a portable desalination unit.

## Practical Tips for Water Management

Managing your water resources effectively involves planning, regular maintenance, and practical know-how.

### Regular Maintenance and Inspections

To ensure the longevity and effectiveness of your water storage and purification systems, establish a routine for regular maintenance and inspections.

### Monthly Checks:

- Inspect all containers for signs of pests or spoilage.

- Ensure all seals are intact and airtight.

- Check expiration dates and rotate items as necessary.

### Bi-Annual Inventory:

- Conduct a thorough inventory check every six months.

- Update your inventory list to reflect current supplies.

- Discard and replace any expired or compromised items.

### Annual Review:

- Reevaluate your stockpile based on any changes in dietary needs or family size.

- Consider adding new items or replacing those that are no longer necessary.

- Ensure all non-food items are in good working condition and replenish as needed.

## Educational Resources and Continued Learning

Staying informed and continually learning about water storage and purification techniques is vital. Utilize resources such as books, online courses, and community workshops to keep your knowledge up to date.

- **Books**: Invest in reputable guides on water storage and purification.

- **Online Courses**: Many organizations offer online classes on water management and purification methods.

- **Community Workshops**: Participate in local workshops and seminars to learn from experts and share knowledge with others.

## Community and Networking

Engage with your community to build a support network. Sharing knowledge, resources, and experiences can strengthen your preparedness efforts.

- **Local Groups**: Join local preparedness or homesteading groups to exchange ideas and resources.

- **Social Media**: Follow water management and preparedness accounts for tips, updates, and community support.

## Practical Water Use Tips

Efficient water use is essential in any survival situation. Here are some practical tips to conserve and make the most of your water supply:

## Water Rationing

In a prolonged emergency, rationing water becomes necessary.

- **Daily Allowance**: Allocate a daily allowance of water per person.

- **Priority Use**: Prioritize drinking and cooking over other uses.

## Recycling Water

Recycling water can significantly extend your supply.

- **Greywater**: Use greywater (from washing dishes and clothes) for flushing toilets and watering plants.

- **Rainwater**: Collect and use rainwater for non-drinking purposes after minimal filtration.

## Hygiene Practices

Maintaining hygiene while conserving water is possible with some adjustments.

- **Hand Sanitizers**: Use hand sanitizers to reduce the need for washing hands with water.

- **Sponge Baths**: Take sponge baths instead of full showers to save water.

## Cooking Tips

Minimize water use in cooking without compromising nutrition.

- **One-Pot Meals**: Cook one-pot meals to reduce water used in cooking and cleaning.

- **Steam Vegetables**: Steam vegetables using minimal water, and use the remaining water in soups or sauces.

Water survival is a critical aspect of any emergency preparedness plan. By understanding and implementing effective water storage solutions and purification methods, you can ensure a reliable supply of clean water for you and your family. Whether you are facing short-term emergencies, long-term disruptions, or evacuation situations, the strategies and techniques outlined in this chapter will help you stay prepared and resilient. Regular maintenance, ongoing education, and efficient water use practices will further enhance your readiness to face any water-related challenges.

# CHAPTER 4
# FORTIFYING YOUR HOME

## Home Security Enhancements

In uncertain times, ensuring the security of your home becomes paramount. Enhancing home security involves a comprehensive approach, addressing vulnerabilities from the perimeter to the core. This chapter explores strategies and techniques to bolster your home's defenses and create a safe haven.

### Perimeter Security

The first layer of home security is the perimeter. Effective perimeter security serves as a deterrent and the first line of defense against intruders.

### Fencing and Gates

### Fencing:

- **Material Selection:** Choose robust materials such as wood, metal, or vinyl. Each has its benefits; metal is durable, wood offers privacy, and vinyl is low maintenance.

- **Height and Design:** Ensure the fence is high enough (at least 6 feet) to deter climbing. Avoid designs that provide handholds or footholds.

**Gates:**

- **Robust Construction:** Install gates that match the strength and durability of your fence. Metal gates are particularly strong and durable.

- **Automation:** Consider automated gates with security keypads or remote controls for added convenience and security.

- **Secure Locks:** Use high-quality locks to secure gates. Multiple locking points add extra security.

## Lighting

Proper lighting is crucial for deterring intruders and enhancing visibility around your home.

### Exterior Lighting:

- **Motion-Sensor Lights:** Install motion-sensor lights that activate when motion is detected. This sudden illumination can startle intruders and draw attention to their presence.

- **Strategic Placement:** Position lights at entry points, around the perimeter, and in dark corners to eliminate hiding spots.

### Pathway Lighting:

- **Continuous Illumination:** Use pathway lights to illuminate walkways and driveways. Solar-powered options are eco-friendly and cost-effective.

- **Design and Functionality:** Choose lights that enhance your home's aesthetics while providing adequate illumination.

## Landscaping

Thoughtful landscaping can enhance security by reducing hiding spots and creating physical barriers.

### Trimmed Shrubs:

- **Visibility:** Keep shrubs and trees trimmed, especially near windows and doors, to eliminate potential hiding spots for intruders.

- **Access Prevention:** Ensure that trees and shrubs do not provide easy access to upper levels of your home.

### Defensive Plants:

- **Thorny Bushes:** Plant thorny bushes like roses or barberry under windows. These act as natural deterrents to intruders.

- **Strategic Planting:** Place defensive plants in vulnerable areas such as under ground-floor windows and along fences.

## Doors and Windows

Doors and windows are common entry points for intruders. Reinforcing these points is essential for home security.

### Doors

### Solid Core Doors:

- **Material:** Use solid core or metal doors for all exterior entrances. These materials provide a robust barrier against forced entry.

- **Installation:** Ensure doors are properly installed with reinforced frames to prevent tampering.

## Locks:

- **Deadbolt Locks:** Install high-quality deadbolt locks that extend at least one inch into the door frame.

- **Strike Plates:** Reinforce strike plates with long screws that penetrate deep into the door frame for added strength.

## Door Reinforcement Kits:

- **Additional Support:** Use door reinforcement kits that provide extra support to the door and frame, making it harder to force entry.

- **Components:** These kits typically include metal bars or plates that reinforce the area around the lock and hinges.

## Advanced Door Security:

- **Smart Locks:** Install smart locks that can be controlled via smartphone apps, providing remote access and monitoring.

- **Doorbell Cameras:** Equip doors with smart doorbells featuring cameras and two-way audio, allowing you to see and communicate with visitors remotely.

## Windows

## Window Locks:

- **Types:** Use reliable locks on all windows, including key-operated locks for added security.

- **Regular Maintenance:** Check and maintain locks regularly to ensure they are functioning properly.

**Security Film:**

- **Application:** Apply security film to windows to make them shatter-resistant. This film holds the glass together even when broken, preventing easy access.

- **Variety:** Available in different thicknesses and levels of protection, choose a film that suits your security needs.

**Window Bars:**

- **Design:** Install decorative window bars that enhance security without compromising the aesthetics of your home.

- **Secure Installation:** Ensure the bars are securely attached to the window frame and cannot be easily removed.

**Glass Break Sensors:**

- **Function:** Install sensors that trigger alarms if a window is broken. These sensors can be integrated into a larger security system for comprehensive protection.

**Alarm Systems**

An effective alarm system is a critical component of home security. It serves as a deterrent and provides immediate alerts in case of unauthorized entry.

**Types of Alarms**

**Monitored Alarms:**

- **Professional Monitoring:** These systems are connected to a monitoring service that contacts authorities in case of a breach.

- **Rapid Response:** Monitored alarms offer faster response times due to immediate notification to law enforcement or security companies.

**Unmonitored Alarms:**

- **Self-Monitoring:** These systems trigger loud sirens to scare off intruders and alert occupants.

- **Cost-Effective:** Generally less expensive than monitored systems, but they require the homeowner to take action when an alarm sounds.

**Components**

**Door and Window Sensors:**

- **Placement:** Install sensors on all doors and windows to detect when they are opened or tampered with.

- **Integration:** Connect these sensors to the main alarm system for immediate alerts.

**Motion Detectors:**

- **Coverage:** Place motion detectors in key areas inside the home to detect movement.

- **Types:** Choose from infrared sensors, microwave sensors, or dual-technology sensors that combine both methods for enhanced accuracy.

**Security Cameras:**

- **Surveillance:** Use cameras to monitor the exterior and interior of your home. Modern systems offer remote viewing via smartphones.

- **Strategic Placement:** Position cameras at entry points, driveways, and other critical areas for comprehensive coverage.

## Safe Rooms

A safe room provides a secure place to retreat in case of an emergency, such as a home invasion or natural disaster.

### Designing a Safe Room

### Location:

- **Interior Room:** Choose an interior room with no windows, such as a basement or large closet. This reduces vulnerability to break-ins.

- **Accessibility:** Ensure the room is easily accessible to all family members in case of an emergency.

### Reinforcement:

- **Walls:** Reinforce walls with steel or Kevlar panels to withstand forced entry.

- **Door:** Install a solid core or metal door with reinforced hinges and a deadbolt lock for maximum security.

### Supplies:

- **Essentials:** Stock the room with water, non-perishable food, a first aid kit, and communication devices.

- **Comfort Items:** Include blankets, pillows, and other items to ensure comfort during extended stays.

**Ventilation:**

- **Air Quality:** Ensure the room has proper ventilation to maintain air quality.

- **Emergency Power:** Consider a backup power source for ventilation systems and essential devices.

## Fortification Techniques

Beyond basic security enhancements, fortifying your home involves structural modifications and advanced techniques to withstand various threats.

### Reinforcing Entry Points

Strengthening entry points makes it more difficult for intruders to gain access.

**Door Frames:**

- **Metal Frames:** Replace wooden door frames with metal ones for added strength and durability.

- **Security Hinges:** Use security hinges that cannot be removed from the outside to prevent tampering.

**Windows:**

- **Polycarbonate Panels:** Replace traditional glass with polycarbonate panels, which are virtually unbreakable and provide excellent security.

- **Window Shutters:** Install roll-down shutters that can be secured from the inside to provide an additional layer of protection.

## Structural Reinforcements

Fortifying the structure of your home can protect against natural disasters and forced entry.

### Walls:

- **Concrete Reinforcement:** Reinforce walls with concrete or cinder blocks to make them more resistant to break-ins and severe weather.

- **Steel Reinforcement:** Add steel rods or mesh to walls for additional strength and security.

### Roof:

- **Hurricane Straps:** Use hurricane straps to secure the roof to the walls, preventing it from being lifted off in high winds.

- **Impact-Resistant Shingles:** Install impact-resistant shingles to protect against hail and debris during storms.

### Foundation:

- **Flood Barriers:** Install flood barriers around the foundation to prevent water from entering your home during floods.

- **Seismic Upgrades:** If you live in an earthquake-prone area, consider seismic retrofitting to strengthen the foundation and increase stability.

## Advanced Security Systems

Incorporating advanced security systems can provide comprehensive protection and peace of mind.

## Smart Home Technology

## Automated Lighting:

- **Control:** Use smart lighting systems to control lights remotely and create the illusion of occupancy when you're not home.

- **Integration:** Integrate smart lighting with your home security system for automated responses to security breaches.

## Smart Locks:

- **Access Control:** Install smart locks that can be controlled via smartphone, allowing you to lock and unlock doors remotely.

- **Monitoring:** Receive alerts when doors are locked or unlocked, providing real-time security updates.

## Integrated Security Systems:

- **Centralized Control:** Integrate alarms, cameras, and sensors into a single smart home system for centralized control and monitoring.

- **Automation:** Automate responses such as turning on lights, locking doors, and activating alarms when a security breach is detected.

## Surveillance Drones

## Drones:

- **Patrolling:** Use drones equipped with cameras to patrol the perimeter of your property. They can provide real-time video feeds and cover areas not easily visible from the ground.

**Integration:** Integrate dronesLet's focus on writing original, detailed content for Chapter 4. I'll ensure the content is unique and comprehensive.

# CHAPTER 5
# OFF-GRID ENERGY
# SOLUTIONS

## Alternative Energy Sources

As we move towards a more sustainable future, alternative energy sources are becoming increasingly vital, especially for those living off-grid. This chapter delves into various alternative energy sources, their benefits, and how to implement them in your off-grid lifestyle.

### Solar Power

Solar power is one of the most popular and accessible forms of alternative energy. It harnesses the sun's energy through photovoltaic (PV) panels, converting sunlight into electricity.

### Benefits:

- **Renewable:** Solar energy is abundant and renewable, available as long as the sun shines.

- **Low Maintenance:** Solar panels require minimal maintenance once installed.

- **Scalable:** Systems can be scaled to meet different energy needs, from small setups for individual appliances to larger systems powering entire homes.

**Implementation:**

1. **Assessment:** Evaluate your energy needs and the solar potential of your location. Factors like sunlight hours, shading, and roof orientation are crucial.

2. **System Design:** Design a system that includes solar panels, inverters, batteries, and charge controllers. Panels can be mounted on rooftops or ground-mounted.

3. **Installation:** Professional installation ensures optimal performance and safety. DIY installation is possible but requires electrical knowledge.

4. **Monitoring and Maintenance:** Regularly monitor system performance and clean panels to maintain efficiency.

**Wind Power**

Wind power is another viable off-grid energy solution. It converts kinetic energy from wind into electricity using wind turbines.

**Benefits:**

- **Renewable:** Wind is a consistent and renewable energy source.

- **Efficient:** Wind turbines can generate significant power, especially in windy areas.

- **Complementary:** Wind power can complement solar power, providing energy during cloudy days or at night.

**Implementation:**

1. **Site Assessment:** Determine wind potential by measuring wind speeds at different heights. Open, unobstructed areas are ideal.

2. **Turbine Selection:** Choose a turbine based on your energy needs and wind conditions. Options range from small turbines for personal use to larger, more powerful units.

3. **Installation:** Proper installation is critical. Turbines must be securely mounted on towers, and connections to your electrical system must be safely made.

4. **Maintenance:** Regular maintenance includes checking for wear, lubricating moving parts, and ensuring electrical connections are intact.

## Hydropower

Hydropower uses flowing or falling water to generate electricity. It's particularly effective for properties near rivers or streams.

**Benefits:**

- **Constant Supply:** Hydropower can provide a constant energy supply if water flow is consistent.

- **Efficient:** Small-scale hydropower systems can generate significant power.

- **Minimal Environmental Impact:** Properly designed systems have minimal impact on the environment.

## Implementation:

1. **Site Assessment:** Evaluate the water source, flow rate, and head (height difference through which water falls). These factors determine potential energy output.

2. **System Design:** Design a system that includes a waterwheel or turbine, generator, and necessary electrical components.

3. **Installation:** Install the system with care to avoid disrupting the waterway. Ensure all connections are secure and waterproof.

4. **Maintenance:** Regularly inspect for debris, wear, and ensure the water flow remains unobstructed.

## Biomass Energy

Biomass energy uses organic materials, such as wood, agricultural residues, and animal waste, to produce heat or electricity.

## Benefits:

- **Renewable:** Biomass is abundant and can be replenished sustainably.

- **Versatile:** Biomass can be used for heating, electricity, and even biofuel production.

- **Carbon Neutral:** When managed sustainably, biomass energy has a low carbon footprint.

## Implementation:

1. **Material Sourcing:** Identify reliable sources of biomass, such as wood chips, crop residues, or animal manure.

2. **System Design:** Design a system suitable for your energy needs. Options include biomass stoves for heating and biomass gasifiers for electricity generation.

3. **Installation:** Install the biomass system following safety guidelines. Ensure proper ventilation to manage emissions.

4. **Maintenance:** Regularly clean and inspect the system to ensure efficient operation. Manage fuel supply sustainably.

## Geothermal Energy

Geothermal energy harnesses heat from the earth, which can be used for heating and electricity.

**Benefits:**

- **Constant Supply:** Geothermal energy is available year-round, unaffected by weather conditions.

- **Efficient:** Geothermal systems are highly efficient, providing consistent energy.

- **Low Emissions:** Geothermal energy has a low environmental impact and minimal emissions.

**Implementation:**

1. **Site Assessment:** Evaluate the geothermal potential of your location. This typically involves drilling to access underground heat.

2. **System Design:** Design a geothermal system that includes heat pumps, underground loops, and necessary electrical components.

3.  **Installation:** Professional installation is recommended due to the complexity of drilling and system integration.

4.  **Maintenance:** Regularly inspect and maintain the system to ensure efficient operation and longevity.

## Energy Conservation Tips

While alternative energy sources are crucial, conserving energy is equally important to maximize efficiency and sustainability.

### Efficient Appliances

Using energy-efficient appliances reduces overall energy consumption, extending the lifespan of your alternative energy system.

### Selection:

- **Energy Star Ratings:** Choose appliances with high energy star ratings for maximum efficiency.

- **Appropriate Sizing:** Select appliances sized appropriately for your needs. Oversized appliances consume more energy unnecessarily.

### Usage:

- **Smart Usage:** Turn off appliances when not in use and unplug devices to avoid standby power consumption.

- **Maintenance:** Regularly maintain appliances to ensure they operate efficiently.

## Insulation and Weatherproofing

Proper insulation and weatherproofing reduce energy loss, making your home more efficient.

### Insulation:

- **Materials:** Use high-quality insulation materials in walls, roofs, and floors.

- **Installation:** Ensure insulation is installed correctly to avoid gaps and maximize effectiveness.

### Weatherproofing:

- **Sealing:** Seal windows, doors, and any other openings to prevent drafts and energy loss.

- **Double Glazing:** Install double-glazed windows to improve thermal efficiency.

## Efficient Lighting

Efficient lighting reduces energy consumption and extends the life of your energy system.

### LED Lighting:

- **Energy Savings:** LED lights consume significantly less energy compared to incandescent bulbs.

- **Longevity:** LEDs have a longer lifespan, reducing the need for frequent replacements.

### Natural Lighting:

- **Daylighting:** Use natural light during the day to reduce reliance on artificial lighting.

- **Skylights:** Install skylights or light tubes to increase natural lighting in your home.

## Behavior Adjustments

Small changes in daily behavior can lead to significant energy savings.

## Thermostat Management:

- **Smart Thermostats:** Use smart thermostats to regulate heating and cooling efficiently.

- **Temperature Settings:** Set your thermostat to energy-saving temperatures, especially when you're away from home.

## Water Usage:

- **Low-Flow Fixtures:** Install low-flow showerheads and faucets to reduce water heating energy.

- **Efficient Water Heating:** Use energy-efficient water heaters and insulate hot water pipes.

## Renewable Energy Storage

Storing renewable energy ensures you have a reliable supply even when generation is low.

## Battery Storage

Battery storage systems store excess energy generated by solar, wind, or other renewable sources for use when generation is insufficient.

## Types of Batteries:

- **Lead-Acid:** Traditional and cost-effective, but with shorter lifespans and lower efficiency.

- **Lithium-Ion:** More efficient, longer-lasting, and increasingly affordable.

## System Design:

- **Capacity:** Choose a battery system with sufficient capacity to meet your energy needs.

- **Integration:** Integrate the battery system with your renewable energy sources and home energy system.

## Maintenance:

- **Regular Checks:** Monitor battery health and performance regularly.

- **Temperature Control:** Ensure batteries are stored in a temperature-controlled environment to maximize lifespan.

## Thermal Storage

Thermal storage systems store heat energy for later use, providing an efficient way to manage energy needs.

## Types of Systems:

- **Water Tanks:** Store hot water generated by solar or biomass systems.

- **Phase Change Materials:** Use materials that absorb and release heat at specific temperatures.

## Implementation:

- **System Design:** Design a thermal storage system that meets your heating and hot water needs.

- **Integration:** Integrate the system with your existing heating and energy systems.

**Maintenance:**

- **Regular Inspections:** Check for leaks and ensure the system is functioning efficiently.

- **Temperature Management:** Maintain optimal temperatures to ensure efficient energy storage and release.

**Conclusion**

Transitioning to off-grid energy solutions requires careful planning and implementation. By harnessing alternative energy sources and adopting energy conservation practices, you can create a sustainable and resilient energy system for your home. Embrace these strategies to enhance your self-sufficiency and reduce your environmental footprint, ensuring a secure and energy-efficient future.

# CHAPTER 6
# STAYING CONNECTED
# DURING A CRISIS

In the face of a crisis, maintaining communication can be the difference between safety and peril. When traditional communication networks fail, having reliable emergency communication devices is crucial. This section explores various tools and strategies to ensure you stay connected during emergencies.

## Emergency Communication Devices

When a storm hits, the power goes out, and cell towers are down, having the right emergency communication devices is essential for receiving critical information and staying in touch with loved ones.

### Hand-Crank Radios

Hand-crank radios are among the most dependable devices during a crisis. Compact and sturdy, these radios don't rely on external power sources. With just a few cranks, they generate enough power to receive broadcasts, invaluable for receiving emergency alerts and updates.

### Features to Look For:

- **Multiple Power Sources:** Hand-crank, solar, and battery options ensure versatility.

- **AM/FM and NOAA Channels:** Access to a variety of frequencies for emergency broadcasts.

- **Built-In Flashlight:** Additional functionality for navigating in the dark.

Hand-crank radios are relatively simple to use. Imagine waking up to find a severe weather warning on the radio, allowing you to prepare adequately before the storm hits. The convenience of having multiple power options ensures you are never left without vital information.

## Two-Way Radios

Two-way radios, also known as walkie-talkies, provide direct communication between parties. In a situation where cell towers are inoperable, these devices become lifelines.

## Key Advantages:

- **Direct Communication:** No reliance on external networks.

- **Range:** Depending on the model, they can cover several miles.

- **Durability:** Often designed to withstand harsh conditions.

Imagine coordinating with family members or neighbors during an evacuation. Two-way radios enable clear and instant communication, ensuring everyone is informed and safe. For example, during a wildfire, you can keep in touch with loved ones even when separated, guiding them to safety.

## Satellite Phones

When local networks fail, satellite phones step in. These devices communicate directly with satellites, providing coverage even in the most remote areas.

**Benefits:**

- **Global Coverage:** Stay connected anywhere in the world.

- **Reliable:** Operates independently of local infrastructure.

- **Emergency Services:** Many models have SOS functions for immediate assistance.

Think of being stranded in the wilderness with no cell service. A satellite phone can be a lifeline, allowing you to call for help regardless of your location. Whether you are sailing in the open sea or hiking in the mountains, satellite phones ensure you are never truly isolated.

**Personal Locator Beacons (PLBs)**

For those who venture into remote areas, Personal Locator Beacons (PLBs) are indispensable. These devices send distress signals to search and rescue satellites, pinpointing your location.

**Key Features:**

- **GPS Positioning:** Accurate location data for rescue teams.

- **Ease of Use:** Simple activation in emergencies.

- **Durability:** Designed to function in extreme conditions.

Imagine hiking in a remote mountain range and sustaining an injury. Activating your PLB ensures that rescue teams can locate and assist you quickly. This technology has saved countless lives, providing peace of mind for adventurers.

## Using Emergency Communication Devices Effectively

Having the right devices is just the beginning; knowing how to use them effectively is equally important. Here are some tips for maximizing the utility of your emergency communication devices:

### Regular Maintenance and Testing

Ensure your devices are in working order by performing regular maintenance and testing.

### Steps to Take:

- **Battery Checks:** Regularly check and replace batteries as needed.

- **Signal Testing:** Periodically test the signal range of two-way radios and satellite phones.

- **Software Updates:** Keep devices updated with the latest firmware or software to ensure optimal performance.

Regular maintenance ensures that your devices are ready to function when you need them most. Imagine discovering a dead battery or a faulty signal during an actual emergency—preventive checks can avert such issues.

### Familiarization and Training

Familiarize yourself and your family with the operation of each device. Conduct training sessions to ensure everyone knows how to use them properly.

### Training Tips:

- **Hands-On Practice:** Allow each family member to practice using the devices.

- **Scenarios:** Simulate different emergency scenarios to practice communication strategies.

- **Instructions:** Keep clear, written instructions with each device for quick reference.

Imagine a family member struggling to use a two-way radio during an emergency due to lack of familiarity. Regular practice ensures everyone can use the devices confidently and effectively.

## Strategic Placement and Accessibility

Strategically place your communication devices in easily accessible locations. Ensure they are readily available when needed.

## Placement Tips:

- **Central Locations:** Store devices in central, easy-to-reach locations within your home.

- **Emergency Kits:** Include communication devices in your emergency kits.

- **Accessibility:** Ensure all family members know where the devices are stored.

Imagine having to search for a device during a time-sensitive emergency. Strategic placement ensures quick access, facilitating prompt communication and response.

## Additional Emergency Communication Tools

In addition to primary communication devices, several supplementary tools can enhance your communication capabilities during a crisis.

## Emergency Whistles

Emergency whistles are simple yet effective tools for signaling for help. They are particularly useful in scenarios where voice communication may be difficult.

### Benefits:

- **Attention-Grabbing:** Loud sound can attract attention from rescuers.

- **Durability:** Designed to withstand harsh conditions.

- **Ease of Use:** Simple and reliable in emergency situations.

Imagine being trapped under debris after an earthquake. Blowing an emergency whistle can alert rescuers to your location, increasing your chances of being found.

## Signal Mirrors

Signal mirrors can be used to reflect sunlight and create visual signals to attract attention from long distances.

### Key Features:

- **Long-Range Visibility:** Can be seen from miles away under the right conditions.

- **Lightweight:** Easy to carry and use.

- **Simple Operation:** Requires minimal training to use effectively.

Imagine being stranded in an open field or on a mountainside. A signal mirror can help you communicate your location to rescuers or passing aircraft.

## Mobile Apps for Emergency Communication

Several mobile apps are designed to facilitate communication during emergencies. These apps can provide critical information and connect you with emergency services.

**Popular Apps:**

- **Zello:** Turns your smartphone into a walkie-talkie.

- **Red Cross Emergency:** Provides real-time alerts and information on emergency situations.

- **Life360:** Allows family members to share locations and communicate during emergencies.

Imagine using a mobile app to receive real-time updates on a natural disaster, helping you make informed decisions to stay safe.

Staying connected during a crisis is paramount for safety and coordination. By investing in reliable emergency communication devices and familiarizing yourself with their use, you can ensure that you and your loved ones remain informed and connected, no matter the situation. From hand-crank radios to satellite phones, each device plays a crucial role in maintaining communication lines when it matters most. Regular maintenance, strategic placement, and hands-on training further enhance your preparedness, enabling you to respond swiftly and effectively in any emergency scenario.

# Establishing Communication Networks

Establishing robust communication networks is crucial for community resilience in the face of crises. These networks ensure that information flows smoothly, even during widespread outages, and help maintain order and safety. This section delves into various strategies and tools for creating and maintaining effective communication networks.

## Family Communication Plans

Start with a family communication plan. This plan ensures that all family members know how to contact each other and where to meet in case of separation.

## Components of a Good Plan:

- **Emergency Contacts:** A list of key contacts, including family, friends, and emergency services.

- **Meeting Points:** Designate specific locations where family members can regroup.

- **Communication Methods:** Primary and secondary communication methods, such as phone, text, and email.

Imagine a scenario where a natural disaster strikes while your family is scattered across town. A pre-established plan ensures that everyone knows how to reconnect and regroup safely.

## Creating the Plan:

1. **Compile Contacts:** Gather contact information for each family member and important emergency services.

2. **Designate Meeting Points:** Choose both local and regional meeting points in case one is inaccessible.

3. **Determine Methods:** Decide on the primary and secondary methods of communication, such as text messages, phone calls, or emails.

Having a clear, written plan that everyone in the family is familiar with can significantly reduce panic and confusion during emergencies.

**Neighborhood Networks**

Building a neighborhood network enhances community resilience. Imagine neighbors working together to share information and resources during a crisis.

**Steps to Establish a Network:**

- **Community Meetings:** Regular meetings to discuss emergency plans and resources.

- **Contact Lists:** A shared list of contact information for quick communication.

- **Roles and Responsibilities:** Assign specific roles, such as coordinators and first responders.

Neighborhood networks foster a sense of community and collective security. For example, during a prolonged power outage, neighbors can pool resources, ensuring everyone has access to essentials like food, water, and information.

**Steps to Implement:**

1. **Organize Meetings:** Hold regular meetings to establish the network and discuss plans.

2. **Create Contact Lists:** Compile a list of contact information for each household.

3. **Assign Roles:** Designate roles and responsibilities to ensure efficient communication and resource distribution.

By working together, neighbors can support each other and create a stronger, more resilient community.

## Community Communication Hubs

Establishing community communication hubs can significantly enhance the effectiveness of local emergency responses. These hubs can serve as centralized points for information dissemination and coordination.

### Key Elements of a Communication Hub:

- **Location:** A central, easily accessible location such as a community center or school.

- **Equipment:** Radios, satellite phones, computers, and other communication devices.

- **Staff:** Trained volunteers or staff to manage the hub and assist with communications.

### Steps to Establish a Hub:

1. **Identify a Location:** Choose a central location that is accessible to the majority of the community.

2. **Equip the Hub:** Stock the hub with necessary communication devices and supplies.

3. **Train Volunteers:** Recruit and train volunteers to manage the hub and assist during emergencies.

Community hubs can provide a reliable source of information and coordination during crises, ensuring that residents stay informed and connected.

## Amateur Radio (Ham Radio)

Ham radio operators play a critical role in emergency communications. These radios can operate independently of local infrastructure, providing reliable communication channels.

### Advantages of Ham Radio:

- **Wide Range:** Communicate over long distances, even internationally.

- **Reliability:** Operates during power outages and network failures.

- **Community Support:** A network of operators ready to assist in emergencies.

Imagine a scenario where traditional communication methods are down, but ham radio operators are still able to relay vital information and coordinate rescue efforts. Joining a local ham radio club and obtaining a license can be a valuable addition to your emergency preparedness toolkit.

### Steps to Get Started:

1. **Join a Club:** Find a local ham radio club and attend meetings to learn more.

2. **Get Licensed:** Study for and obtain a ham radio license.

3. **Practice Regularly:** Participate in regular drills and exercises to maintain proficiency.

Ham radio networks can provide a crucial communication lifeline during emergencies, connecting communities and facilitating coordinated responses.

## Social Media and Online Platforms

In today's digital age, social media and online platforms are powerful tools for communication during a crisis. Platforms like Twitter, Facebook, and WhatsApp can disseminate information quickly and reach a broad audience.

### Effective Use of Social Media:

- **Real-Time Updates:** Share real-time updates and alerts.

- **Community Engagement:** Engage with community members and share resources.

- **Verification:** Ensure information is accurate and verified to avoid spreading misinformation.

Imagine using social media to check in with loved ones, share safety updates, and find local resources. Even in times of crisis, these platforms can be invaluable for staying informed and connected.

### Steps to Utilize Social Media:

1. **Create Accounts:** Ensure that you and your family members have accounts on major social media platforms.

2. **Follow Authorities:** Follow local emergency services, news outlets, and government agencies for real-time updates.

3. **Engage and Share:** Use social media to communicate with your network and share important information.

By leveraging social media, you can enhance your ability to stay informed and connected during emergencies.

## Public Information Systems

Public information systems, such as emergency alert systems and community notification services, play a crucial role in disseminating information during crises.

## Types of Systems:

- **Emergency Alert Systems (EAS):** Broadcasts emergency alerts via radio, television, and other media.

- **Reverse 911 Systems:** Sends automated messages to residents' phones with emergency information.

- **Community Notification Services:** Uses email, text, and voice messages to inform residents about emergencies.

## Implementing Public Information Systems:

1. **Register for Alerts:** Ensure you and your family are registered for local emergency alert services.

2. **Stay Informed:** Pay attention to alerts and follow instructions from local authorities.

3. **Spread the Word:** Encourage neighbors and community members to register for alerts.

Public information systems can provide timely and accurate information during emergencies, helping you stay safe and informed.

## Building Redundant Communication Networks

Creating a resilient communication system involves combining various devices and networks to ensure redundancy. This way, if one method fails, others can still function, keeping you connected.

**Redundancy and Backup Systems:**

- **Multiple Devices:** Invest in various communication devices to cover different scenarios.

- **Power Sources:** Ensure devices have multiple power sources, such as batteries, solar, and hand-crank options.

- **Regular Testing:** Regularly test all devices and systems to ensure they work when needed.

Imagine having a layered communication system. If your cell phone fails, you can fall back on a two-way radio, and if that fails, a satellite phone or PLB is your next line of defense.

**Steps to Build Resilience:**

1. **Diversify Devices:** Acquire different types of communication devices, such as radios, phones, and beacons.

2. **Ensure Power Options:** Equip each device with multiple power sources.

3. **Test Regularly:** Conduct regular tests to ensure each device is functional.

By building redundant communication networks, you can ensure that you remain connected and informed, regardless of the circumstances.

Establishing robust communication networks is essential for maintaining safety and order during emergencies. From family communication plans and neighborhood networks to community hubs and ham radio systems, there are numerous strategies and tools available to ensure effective communication. By leveraging these resources and building redundant networks, you can enhance your resilience and preparedness, ensuring that you and your community stay connected and informed in any crisis.

# CHAPTER 7
# ESSENTIAL HOME
# MEDICINES

Maintaining a well-stocked home medicine cabinet is crucial for handling common ailments, minor injuries, and chronic conditions. This section will cover essential medications, their uses, dosages, precautions, and tips for proper storage.

## Essential Medications

### 1. Pain Relievers

### Acetaminophen (Tylenol)

- **Uses**: Reduces fever and alleviates mild to moderate pain such as headaches, muscle aches, and toothaches.

- **Dosage**: Follow label instructions based on age and weight.

- **Precautions**: Do not exceed the recommended dose to avoid liver damage.

### Ibuprofen (Advil, Motrin)

- **Uses**: Treats inflammation, fever, and pain from conditions like arthritis, menstrual cramps, and minor injuries.

- **Dosage**: Typically taken every 4-6 hours as needed.

- **Precautions**: Can cause stomach upset; take with food or milk to minimize this effect.

## Aspirin

- **Uses**: Reduces fever, pain, and inflammation; also used in low doses to prevent blood clots.

- **Dosage**: Follow label instructions; low-dose aspirin is often used daily for heart attack prevention.

- **Precautions**: Not recommended for children due to the risk of Reye's syndrome.

## Naproxen (Aleve)

- **Uses**: Relieves inflammation, pain, and stiffness caused by conditions like arthritis, muscle aches, and menstrual cramps.

- **Dosage**: Typically taken every 8-12 hours as needed.

- **Precautions**: Can cause stomach upset; take with food or milk to minimize this effect. Consult a doctor if you have certain heart conditions.

## Topical Analgesics (Icy Hot, Bengay)

- **Uses**: Provides temporary relief from muscle and joint pain through a warming or cooling sensation.

- **Dosage**: Apply a thin layer to the affected area up to four times daily.

- **Precautions**: For external use only; avoid contact with eyes and mucous membranes.

## 2. Antihistamines

### Diphenhydramine (Benadryl)

- **Uses**: Treats allergic reactions, hay fever, and cold symptoms; also used as a sleep aid.

- **Dosage**: Typically taken every 4-6 hours as needed.

- **Precautions**: Can cause drowsiness; avoid alcohol and be cautious when driving.

### Loratadine (Claritin)

- **Uses**: Non-drowsy antihistamine for allergy relief.

- **Dosage**: Usually taken once daily.

- **Precautions**: Less likely to cause drowsiness, but still exercise caution with activities requiring alertness.

### Cetirizine (Zyrtec)

- **Uses**: Non-drowsy antihistamine for allergy relief from symptoms like sneezing, itching, and runny nose.

- **Dosage**: Usually taken once daily.

- **Precautions**: While less likely to cause drowsiness, it can still affect alertness in some individuals.

### Fexofenadine (Allegra)

- **Uses**: Non-drowsy antihistamine for relieving symptoms of seasonal allergies.

- **Dosage**: Typically taken once or twice daily.

- **Precautions**: Avoid taking with fruit juices as they can reduce the absorption of the medication.

## 3. Decongestants

### Pseudoephedrine (Sudafed)

- **Uses**: Relieves nasal congestion due to colds, allergies, and sinus infections.

- **Dosage**: Typically taken every 4-6 hours.

- **Precautions**: Can increase heart rate and blood pressure; consult with a doctor if you have heart conditions.

### Oxymetazoline (Afrin)

- **Uses**: Nasal spray for temporary relief of nasal congestion.

- **Dosage**: Usually used every 12 hours.

- **Precautions**: Do not use for more than three days to avoid rebound congestion.

### Phenylephrine (Sudafed PE)

- **Uses**: Relieves nasal congestion from colds, allergies, and sinus infections.

- **Dosage**: Typically taken every 4-6 hours.

- **Precautions**: May cause nervousness, dizziness, or sleeplessness; consult a doctor if you have certain health conditions.

## 4. Digestive Aids

### Loperamide (Imodium)

- **Uses**: Treats diarrhea by slowing down gut movement.

- **Dosage**: Initial higher dose followed by a lower dose after each loose stool.

- **Precautions**: Not for use if you have a high fever or blood in your stools.

### Bismuth Subsalicylate (Pepto-Bismol)

- **Uses**: Treats diarrhea, heartburn, and nausea.

- **Dosage**: Follow label instructions.

- **Precautions**: Can darken the stool and tongue; not for children with viral infections.

### Antacids (Tums, Rolaids)

- **Uses**: Neutralizes stomach acid to relieve heartburn and indigestion.

- **Dosage**: Chew tablets as needed.

- **Precautions**: Overuse can lead to constipation or diarrhea.

### Simethicone (Gas-X)

- **Uses**: Relieves bloating and gas.

- **Dosage**: Usually taken after meals and at bedtime.

- **Precautions**: Generally safe; follow label instructions.

## 5. Topical Medications

### Hydrocortisone Cream

- **Uses**: Reduces inflammation and itching from insect bites, eczema, and rashes.

- **Dosage**: Apply a thin layer to the affected area 1-4 times daily.

- **Precautions**: Do not use on broken skin or for extended periods without consulting a doctor.

### Antibiotic Ointments (Neosporin, Bacitracin)

- **Uses**: Prevents infection in minor cuts, scrapes, and burns.

- **Dosage**: Apply a thin layer to the affected area 1-3 times daily.

- **Precautions**: Avoid using on large areas or deep wounds without medical advice.

### Antifungal Creams (Clotrimazole, Miconazole)

- **Uses**: Treats fungal infections like athlete's foot, jock itch, and ringworm.

- **Dosage**: Apply to the affected area 1-2 times daily.

- **Precautions**: Continue treatment for the full recommended duration, even if symptoms improve.

### Burn Ointments (Aloe Vera, Silver Sulfadiazine)

- **Uses**: Treats minor burns and promotes healing.

- **Dosage**: Apply to the affected area as directed.

- **Precautions**: For external use only; avoid use on large or severe burns without medical advice.

## 6. Cough and Cold Remedies

### Dextromethorphan (Robitussin DM)

- **Uses**: Suppresses dry cough.

- **Dosage**: Follow label instructions; typically taken every 4-6 hours.

- **Precautions**: Do not exceed the recommended dose; can cause dizziness or drowsiness.

### Guaifenesin (Mucinex)

- **Uses**: Expectorant that helps thin and loosen mucus.

- **Dosage**: Usually taken every 4-6 hours with a full glass of water.

- **Precautions**: Stay hydrated to help the medication work effectively.

### Mentholated Rubs (Vicks VapoRub)

- **Uses**: Provides temporary relief from cough and muscle aches.

- **Dosage**: Apply to the chest and throat or affected muscles.

- **Precautions**: For external use only; avoid contact with eyes and mucous membranes.

## 7. Wound Care Supplies

### Sterile Gauze and Bandages

- **Uses**: Protects wounds from infection and aids in healing.

- **Dosage**: Change dressings as needed to keep the wound clean.

- **Precautions**: Ensure hands are clean before changing dressings.

### Adhesive Bandages (Band-Aids)

- **Uses**: Covers small cuts and abrasions.

- **Dosage**: Apply to clean, dry skin.

- **Precautions**: Change bandages regularly to keep the area clean and dry.

### Hydrogen Peroxide

- **Uses**: Cleans minor cuts and scrapes.

- **Dosage**: Apply a small amount to the affected area.

- **Precautions**: Do not use on deep wounds; can damage healthy tissue if overused.

### Rubbing Alcohol

- **Uses**: Disinfects skin and surfaces.

- **Dosage**: Apply to the skin with a cotton ball or pad.

- **Precautions**: Flammable; use in a well-ventilated area away from open flames.

## Butterfly Closures

- **Uses**: Holds edges of small cuts together to promote healing.

- **Dosage**: Apply as needed to clean, dry skin.

- **Precautions**: Ensure proper application to avoid further skin damage.

## 8. Miscellaneous Essentials

### Thermometer

- **Uses**: Measures body temperature to detect fever.

- **Dosage**: Follow instructions for use.

- **Precautions**: Clean before and after use to prevent infection spread.

### Tweezers

- **Uses**: Removes splinters, ticks, and other small foreign objects from the skin.

- **Dosage**: Use as needed.

- **Precautions**: Sterilize before and after each use to prevent infection.

### Scissors

- **Uses**: Cuts bandages, medical tape, and clothing around wounds.

- **Dosage**: Use as needed.

- **Precautions**: Keep scissors clean and sharp; store safely to avoid injury.

## Gloves

- **Uses**: Protects hands when dealing with blood, bodily fluids, or open wounds.

- **Dosage**: Use a new pair for each situation requiring sterile conditions.

- **Precautions**: Dispose of gloves after a single use to prevent cross-contamination.

## Safety Pins

- **Uses**: Secures bandages and slings, temporarily fixes clothing or other fabric needs.

- **Dosage**: Use as needed.

- **Precautions**: Sterilize before use if they will be in contact with wounds.

## Cotton Balls and Swabs

- **Uses**: Applies ointments, cleans wounds, or removes makeup.

- **Dosage**: Use as needed.

- **Precautions**: Store in a dry, clean place to maintain sterility.

## Proper Storage and Maintenance of Home Medicines

Proper storage and maintenance of medications ensure their effectiveness and safety. Here are some tips for keeping your home medicine kit in top condition:

**Storage Tips:**

- **Cool, Dry Place**: Store medications in a cool, dry place away from direct sunlight and moisture.

- **Original Packaging**: Keep medications in their original packaging to preserve expiration dates and usage instructions.

- **Out of Reach**: Store medications out of reach of children and pets to prevent accidental ingestion.

**Maintenance Tips**:

- **Regular Checks**: Periodically check expiration dates and replace expired medications.

- **Organize**: Keep medications organized and labeled for easy identification.

- **Disposal**: Properly dispose of expired or unused medications to prevent misuse. Check local guidelines for safe disposal methods.

**Building a Home Medicine Kit**

Creating a comprehensive home medicine kit involves selecting the right medications and supplies to address common health issues. Here's a guide to building an effective kit:

**Step-by-Step Guide**:

1. **Assess Needs**: Consider the specific health needs of your household, including any chronic conditions or allergies.

2. **Select Essentials**: Choose essential medications and supplies based on your assessment.

3. **Organize**: Arrange the items in a durable, easily accessible container.

4. **Educate**: Ensure all household members know how to use the items in the kit.

**Suggested Contents**:

- **Pain Relievers**: Acetaminophen, ibuprofen, aspirin.

- **Allergy Medications**: Diphenhydramine, loratadine.

- **Digestive Aids**: Loperamide, antacids.

- **Topical Treatments**: Hydrocortisone cream, antibiotic ointments, antifungal creams.

- **Cough and Cold Remedies**: Dextromethorphan, guaifenesin.

- **Wound Care**: Sterile gauze, adhesive bandages, hydrogen peroxide.

- **Miscellaneous Essentials**: Thermometer, tweezers, scissors, gloves.

**Importance of Education and Training**

Having a well-stocked medicine cabinet is essential, but it's equally important that household members are educated on how to use the items properly. Consider these tips for effective education and training:

**Regular Training Sessions**:

- **Practice**: Conduct regular training sessions to practice using the medications and tools in the kit.

- **Scenarios**: Simulate different emergency scenarios to build confidence and competence.

- **Instructions**: Keep clear, written instructions with each item for quick reference.

**Educational Resources**:

- **First Aid Courses**: Enroll in local first aid courses offered by organizations like the Red Cross.

- **Online Tutorials**: Utilize online resources and videos to learn about basic first aid and emergency response.

- **Printed Guides**: Keep first aid manuals and medical guides in the home for reference.

**Expanding Your Medicine Kit for Special Needs**

Depending on the specific needs of your household, you may need to include additional items in your medicine kit. Consider the following:

**Chronic Conditions**:

- **Prescription Medications**: Ensure you have an adequate supply of any necessary prescription medications.

- **Medical Devices**: Include necessary medical devices, such as glucose meters or inhalers.

**Infants and Children**:

- **Pediatric Medications**: Stock age-appropriate medications for common ailments, such as liquid acetaminophen or ibuprofen.

- **Baby Supplies**: Include items like diaper rash ointment and teething gels.

**Elderly Care**:

- **Mobility Aids**: Include items that assist with mobility, such as a walking stick or braces.

- **Hearing and Vision**: Stock extra batteries for hearing aids and spare glasses.

**Pets**:

- **Pet-Specific Medications**: Include any medications or first aid supplies specific to your pets.

- **Veterinary Contact Information**: Keep a list of emergency veterinary contacts.

A well-prepared home medicine cabinet is a cornerstone of household health and safety. By understanding the uses, dosages, and precautions of essential medications and ensuring proper storage and maintenance, you can effectively manage minor ailments and injuries. Building a comprehensive home medicine kit, educating household members, and tailoring the kit to meet specific needs will enhance your ability to respond to medical situations efficiently and confidently. Regular training and keeping up-to-date with first aid practices will ensure that you and your family are always prepared for any health-related emergencies.

## Creating a Home Pharmacy

Establishing a home pharmacy is an essential step towards ensuring that you and your family are prepared for common medical situations, emergencies, and chronic conditions. This section provides a comprehensive guide on setting up a home pharmacy, including selecting medications, organizing the space, and maintaining the inventory.

## Step-by-Step Guide to Creating a Home Pharmacy

### Step 1: Assess Your Needs

Before setting up your home pharmacy, assess the specific medical needs of your household. Consider any chronic conditions, allergies, or special requirements that may dictate the types of medications and supplies you need.

### Considerations:

- **Chronic Conditions**: Stock medications for conditions like diabetes, asthma, hypertension, and heart disease.

- **Allergies**: Include antihistamines, epinephrine injectors (if prescribed), and other allergy medications.

- **Children and Infants**: Ensure you have age-appropriate medications for common illnesses.

- **Elderly**: Consider the specific needs of older adults, including mobility aids and medications for arthritis, osteoporosis, and other age-related conditions.

### Step 2: Select Essential Medications and Supplies

Building on the list of essential medications outlined earlier, ensure your home pharmacy is equipped with a wide range of over-the-counter and prescription medications, as well as necessary medical supplies.

**Essential Medications:**

- **Pain Relievers**: Acetaminophen, ibuprofen, aspirin, naproxen.

- **Allergy Medications**: Diphenhydramine, loratadine, cetirizine, fexofenadine.

- **Digestive Aids**: Loperamide, bismuth subsalicylate, antacids, simethicone.

- **Topical Treatments**: Hydrocortisone cream, antibiotic ointments, antifungal creams, burn ointments.

- **Cough and Cold Remedies**: Dextromethorphan, guaifenesin, mentholated rubs.

**Medical Supplies:**

- **Wound Care**: Sterile gauze, adhesive bandages, hydrogen peroxide, rubbing alcohol, butterfly closures.

- **Miscellaneous**: Thermometer, tweezers, scissors, gloves, cotton balls, safety pins.

**Step 3: Organize Your Home Pharmacy**

Organization is key to ensuring that your home pharmacy is functional and efficient. Proper organization helps you find what you need quickly, especially during emergencies.

**Organizational Tips:**

- **Storage Containers**: Use clear, labeled containers to keep medications and supplies organized.

- **Shelving**: Install shelves to maximize space and keep items within easy reach.

- **Categories**: Group medications and supplies by category (e.g., pain relievers, allergy medications, wound care).

- **Labels**: Clearly label all containers and shelves to ensure easy identification.

**Example Layout:**

- **Top Shelf**: Store items that are rarely used or have long expiration dates.

- **Middle Shelves**: Keep frequently used medications and supplies at eye level for easy access.

- **Bottom Shelf**: Store heavier items or those used less frequently.

**Step 4: Maintain Your Home Pharmacy**

Regular maintenance is crucial to keep your home pharmacy effective and safe. This includes monitoring expiration dates, restocking supplies, and ensuring everything is in working order.

**Maintenance Tips:**

- **Check Expiration Dates**: Regularly go through your medications and supplies to check for expired items. Replace them as needed.

- **Restock Regularly**: Keep an inventory list and update it whenever you use an item. This helps ensure you always have necessary supplies on hand.

- **Cleanliness**: Keep the area clean and free from dust and moisture to maintain the integrity of your medications.

- **Review Needs**: Periodically reassess the medical needs of your household and adjust your inventory accordingly.

## Step 5: Educate Your Household

Ensuring that all household members are knowledgeable about the home pharmacy is crucial. They should know where it is located, what it contains, and how to use the items properly.

## Education Tips:

- **Training Sessions**: Conduct regular training sessions to familiarize everyone with the contents and their uses.

- **Written Instructions**: Keep clear, written instructions with each item to guide proper usage.

- **Emergency Contacts**: Post a list of emergency contacts, including doctors, local hospitals, and poison control centers, in a visible location.

## Enhancing Your Home Pharmacy with Technology

Incorporating technology can greatly enhance the functionality of your home pharmacy. Consider the following tools and resources:

## Digital Inventory Apps:

- **Medication Management Apps**: Use apps like Medisafe or MyMeds to keep track of medication schedules and inventory.

- **Reminders**: Set up reminders for medication dosages and restocking supplies.

**Telehealth Services:**

- **Virtual Consultations**: Use telehealth services for medical consultations, prescription renewals, and advice on using medications.

- **Online Pharmacies**: Order medications and supplies online to ensure you always have what you need without frequent trips to the pharmacy.

**Smart Devices:**

- **Smart Thermometers**: Use digital thermometers with Bluetooth capabilities to track and record temperature readings.

- **Automated Pill Dispensers**: Invest in automated dispensers to manage complex medication schedules, ensuring doses are taken correctly.

**Special Considerations for a Home Pharmacy**

Depending on your household, there may be specific considerations to address when setting up your home pharmacy.

**Infants and Children:**

- **Childproofing**: Ensure all medications and supplies are stored out of reach of children. Use childproof containers and locks.

- **Pediatric Medications**: Include age-appropriate formulations for pain relief, fever reduction, and other common ailments.

**Elderly Care:**

- **Accessibility**: Make sure items are easily accessible for elderly household members. Consider using large print labels.

- **Special Needs**: Stock supplies for common elderly conditions, such as compression stockings for circulation issues or pill organizers for managing multiple medications.

**Pets:**

- **Pet-Specific Medications**: Include medications and supplies specific to your pets' needs.

- **Veterinary Contacts**: Keep a list of emergency veterinary contacts and ensure medications are stored separately from human medications.

Creating a home pharmacy is a proactive step in ensuring the health and safety of your household. By assessing your needs, selecting essential medications and supplies, organizing effectively, maintaining your inventory, and educating your household, you can build a reliable and functional home pharmacy. Incorporating technology and considering special needs further enhances its effectiveness, making sure you are always prepared for any medical situation that arises. Regularly review and update your home pharmacy to keep it current and ready for any health-related emergencies.

# CHAPTER 8
# CRISIS SURVIVAL GEAR

In times of crisis, having the right survival gear can make a significant difference in ensuring your safety and well-being. This chapter explores the must-have gear for various emergency scenarios, focusing on essential items that can help you navigate and survive during crises.

## Must-Have Gear

### 1. Water Filtration and Storage

**Water is the most critical resource during any emergency. Ensuring you have a reliable method for filtering and storing water is paramount.**

### Portable Water Filters

- **Types**: Straw filters, pump filters, gravity filters.

- **Uses**: Removes bacteria, protozoa, and sediment from water sources.

- **Advantages**: Lightweight, easy to use, and effective in providing safe drinking water from natural sources.

### Water Purification Tablets

- **Uses**: Chemical tablets (iodine, chlorine dioxide) to kill pathogens in water.

- **Advantages**: Compact, lightweight, and easy to carry; effective in killing viruses, bacteria, and protozoa.

- **Dosage**: Follow manufacturer instructions; typically one tablet per liter of water.

## Water Storage Containers

- **Types**: Collapsible water bottles, water bladders, large storage tanks.

- **Advantages**: Durable, reusable, and easy to transport; essential for storing purified water.

- **Capacity**: Varies from 1 liter to several gallons; choose based on your needs and available space.

## 2. Food Supplies

**Having a stockpile of non-perishable food ensures that you have enough nourishment during a crisis.**

### Freeze-Dried Meals

- **Advantages**: Lightweight, long shelf-life, easy to prepare with hot water.

- **Variety**: Available in various flavors and dietary options.

### Canned Goods

- **Types**: Vegetables, fruits, meats, beans.

- **Advantages**: Long shelf-life, easy to store, and can be eaten without heating if necessary.

- **Storage Tips**: Store in a cool, dry place and regularly rotate stock to ensure freshness.

## Energy Bars and Snacks

- **Types**: Protein bars, granola bars, nuts, dried fruits.

- **Advantages**: Compact, high-calorie, and easy to consume on the go.

- **Shelf-Life**: Check expiration dates and rotate stock regularly.

## 3. Shelter and Warmth

**Protection from the elements is crucial for survival, especially in extreme weather conditions.**

## Tents and Tarps

- **Types**: Backpacking tents, emergency bivy sacks, waterproof tarps.

- **Uses**: Provides shelter from rain, wind, and cold.

- **Advantages**: Lightweight, compact, and quick to set up.

## Sleeping Bags and Blankets

- **Types**: Down or synthetic sleeping bags, emergency thermal blankets.

- **Advantages**: Provides warmth and comfort during the night.

- **Temperature Ratings**: Choose based on the climate of your region and the expected weather conditions.

## Fire Starting Tools

- **Types**: Waterproof matches, lighters, ferrocerium rods.

- **Uses**: Essential for warmth, cooking, and signaling for help.

- **Advantages**: Reliable and easy to use; ferrocerium rods work in all weather conditions.

## 4. First Aid Kit

**A comprehensive first aid kit is indispensable for treating injuries and medical emergencies.**

### Basic Supplies

- **Items**: Adhesive bandages, gauze pads, antiseptic wipes, medical tape.

- **Uses**: Treats minor cuts, scrapes, and wounds.

### Medications

- **Types**: Pain relievers (acetaminophen, ibuprofen), antihistamines (diphenhydramine), anti-diarrheal (loperamide).

- **Uses**: Alleviates pain, allergic reactions, and gastrointestinal issues.

### Tools and Equipment

- **Items**: Tweezers, scissors, digital thermometer, CPR mask.

- **Uses**: Removes splinters, cuts bandages, measures temperature, provides emergency resuscitation.

## 5. Lighting and Power

**Reliable lighting and power sources are essential for visibility and operating electronic devices during a crisis.**

### Flashlights and Headlamps

- **Types**: LED flashlights, headlamps with adjustable brightness.

- **Advantages**: Long battery life, lightweight, and hands-free operation (headlamps).

- **Power Source**: Use rechargeable batteries or solar-powered options for extended use.

### Portable Chargers and Power Banks

- **Uses**: Keeps essential electronic devices (phones, radios, GPS) charged.

- **Advantages**: High-capacity power banks can charge multiple devices; solar chargers provide a renewable energy source.

- **Capacity**: Choose power banks with at least 10,000 mAh for extended usage.

### Lanterns

- **Types**: LED lanterns, solar-powered lanterns.

- **Advantages**: Provides 360-degree illumination for larger areas; solar-powered options reduce the need for batteries.

## 6. Communication Devices

**Staying informed and being able to communicate with others is vital during emergencies.**

### Two-Way Radios (Walkie-Talkies)

- **Uses**: Allows communication between family members or group members.

- **Advantages**: Works independently of cell networks; useful in remote areas.

- **Range**: Choose models with a range that suits your needs, typically 2-5 miles.

### Emergency Radios

- **Types**: Hand-crank radios, solar-powered radios.

- **Uses**: Receives weather alerts, news updates, and emergency broadcasts.

- **Advantages**: No need for batteries; hand-crank and solar options ensure constant power supply.

### Cell Phones and Satellite Phones

- **Uses**: Primary communication tool; satellite phones for areas with no cell coverage.

- **Advantages**: Allows contact with emergency services and loved ones; satellite phones provide global coverage.

- **Accessories**: Include solar chargers or power banks to keep phones charged.

## 7. Tools and Multi-Tools

**Having versatile tools can help with a variety of tasks, from building shelter to performing repairs.**

### Multi-Tools

- **Types**: Swiss Army knives, Leatherman tools.

- **Features**: Includes knives, pliers, screwdrivers, and other essential tools in one compact device.

- **Uses**: Versatile and useful for a wide range of tasks.

### Fixed-Blade Knives

- **Uses**: Essential for cutting, preparing food, and self-defense.

- **Advantages**: Durable and reliable; choose a high-quality stainless steel blade.

### Shovels and Axes

- **Types**: Collapsible shovels, compact axes.

- **Uses**: Digging, cutting wood, building shelter.

- **Advantages**: Lightweight and portable; essential for outdoor survival scenarios.

## 8. Personal Protection

**Ensuring personal safety and protection is crucial during a crisis.**

### Protective Clothing

- **Types**: Waterproof jackets, insulated gloves, sturdy boots.

- **Uses**: Protects against harsh weather conditions and injuries.

- **Advantages**: Durable and designed for extreme conditions.

## Respiratory Masks

- **Types**: N95 masks, reusable respirators.

- **Uses**: Protects against dust, smoke, and airborne pathogens.

- **Advantages**: Essential for environments with poor air quality.

## Safety Goggles

- **Uses**: Protects eyes from debris, chemicals, and harmful particles.

- **Advantages**: Provides clear vision and safety during hazardous activities.

Equipping yourself with the right crisis survival gear is essential for ensuring safety, comfort, and resilience during emergencies. By carefully selecting and maintaining these must-have items, you can better prepare for any crisis and protect yourself and your loved ones. Regularly update and practice using your gear to ensure you are always ready for any situation.

## Stockpiling Essentials

Preparing for emergencies involves more than just having the right survival gear and first aid supplies; it also requires a well-thought-out stockpile of essential items. Stockpiling ensures that you have the necessary resources to sustain you and your family during extended periods of crisis. This section will cover the essential items you should consider stockpiling, strategies for effective stockpiling, and tips for maintaining your stockpile.

# Essential Items to Stockpile

## 1. Food Supplies

Having a diverse range of non-perishable food items is critical for survival. Focus on items that have a long shelf life, are easy to prepare, and provide essential nutrients.

### Canned Goods

- **Types**: Vegetables, fruits, meats, beans, soups.

- **Advantages**: Long shelf life, easy to store, can be consumed without heating if necessary.

- **Storage Tips**: Rotate stock regularly and check expiration dates to ensure freshness.

### Dry Goods

- **Types**: Rice, pasta, beans, lentils, oats.

- **Advantages**: High in calories and nutrients, versatile for various recipes.

- **Storage Tips**: Store in airtight containers to prevent spoilage and infestation.

### Freeze-Dried and Dehydrated Foods

- **Types**: Fruits, vegetables, meats, full meals.

- **Advantages**: Lightweight, long shelf life, easy to prepare with water.

- **Storage Tips**: Keep in cool, dry places and ensure packaging is intact.

## Cooking Essentials

- **Types**: Cooking oil, salt, sugar, spices.

- **Advantages**: Enhance the flavor and nutritional value of meals.

- **Storage Tips**: Store in sealed containers to prevent contamination.

## 2. Water Supplies

Water is essential for survival, and it's crucial to have a sufficient supply of potable water.

## Bottled Water

- **Advantages**: Convenient and portable.

- **Storage Tips**: Store in a cool, dark place away from direct sunlight and chemicals.

## Water Storage Containers

- **Types**: Large storage tanks, water barrels, collapsible water containers.

- **Advantages**: Store large quantities of water, reusable.

- **Storage Tips**: Clean containers thoroughly before use and treat water with appropriate purification methods.

## Water Purification Supplies

- **Types**: Water filters, purification tablets, bleach.

- **Advantages**: Ensure access to safe drinking water from various sources.

- **Storage Tips**: Keep in a cool, dry place and check expiration dates on chemical purifiers.

## 3. Medical Supplies

Beyond a basic first aid kit, stockpiling additional medical supplies can be lifesaving.

### Over-the-Counter Medications

- **Types**: Pain relievers, antihistamines, anti-diarrheal medications, cold and flu medications.

- **Advantages**: Treat common illnesses and symptoms.

- **Storage Tips**: Store in a cool, dry place and monitor expiration dates.

### Prescription Medications

- **Advantages**: Essential for managing chronic conditions.

- **Storage Tips**: Rotate stock and consult with your healthcare provider about obtaining extra supplies.

### Medical Equipment

- **Types**: Blood pressure monitors, glucose meters, thermometers.

- **Advantages**: Monitor health conditions and track vital signs.

- **Storage Tips**: Keep devices clean and ensure batteries are functional.

## 4. Personal Hygiene Products

Maintaining hygiene is crucial for preventing illness and maintaining morale.

### Sanitation Supplies

- **Types**: Toilet paper, baby wipes, hand sanitizer, soap.

- **Advantages**: Essential for maintaining cleanliness.

- **Storage Tips**: Store in a dry, accessible location.

### Feminine Hygiene Products

- **Types**: Tampons, sanitary pads, menstrual cups.

- **Advantages**: Critical for women's health and comfort.

- **Storage Tips**: Keep in original packaging in a dry place.

### Oral Hygiene Products

- **Types**: Toothbrushes, toothpaste, dental floss.

- **Advantages**: Prevent dental issues and maintain oral health.

- **Storage Tips**: Store in a dry, clean place.

## 5. Household Supplies

Having a variety of household supplies can make surviving a crisis more manageable.

### Cleaning Supplies

- **Types**: Disinfectants, bleach, sponges, paper towels.

- **Advantages**: Prevent the spread of germs and maintain a clean environment.

- **Storage Tips**: Store in a secure place away from food and children.

### Tools and Repair Kits

- **Types**: Multi-tools, duct tape, rope, sewing kits.

- **Advantages**: Useful for repairs and maintenance.

- **Storage Tips**: Keep organized in a tool kit or designated area.

### Lighting and Power Supplies

- **Types**: Batteries, candles, lanterns, solar chargers.

- **Advantages**: Provide light and power during outages.

- **Storage Tips**: Store in a dry place and check battery expiration dates.

### Strategies for Effective Stockpiling

### 1. Inventory Management

- **Track Your Stock**: Maintain an inventory list of all items in your stockpile, including quantities and expiration dates.

- **Rotate Stock**: Use the "first in, first out" method to ensure older items are used before newer ones.

- **Regular Checks**: Conduct regular checks to update your inventory and replace expired or used items.

## 2. Space Optimization

- **Utilize Space Efficiently**: Make use of available space in your home, such as basements, closets, and under beds.

- **Shelving Units**: Install shelves to maximize vertical space and keep items organized.

- **Labeling**: Clearly label all storage containers and shelves for easy identification and access.

## 3. Budgeting

- **Prioritize Needs**: Focus on essential items first and gradually build your stockpile over time.

- **Buy in Bulk**: Purchase non-perishable items in bulk to save money and reduce the frequency of shopping trips.

- **Sales and Coupons**: Take advantage of sales, discounts, and coupons to stock up on essentials.

## 4. Security and Safety

- **Secure Storage**: Ensure your stockpile is stored in a secure location to prevent theft or tampering.

- **Pest Control**: Take measures to protect your stockpile from pests by using airtight containers and maintaining cleanliness.

- **Temperature Control**: Store items in a cool, dry place to extend their shelf life and maintain quality.

## Maintaining Your Stockpile

### 1. Regular Maintenance

- **Update Inventory**: Regularly update your inventory list to reflect items used and new additions.

- **Check Expiration Dates**: Routinely check expiration dates and use or replace items as needed.

- **Restock**: Replace items that have been used or are nearing their expiration dates.

### 2. Practice and Familiarity

- **Use Your Supplies**: Occasionally use items from your stockpile to ensure familiarity with them and to rotate stock.

- **Practice Scenarios**: Conduct practice scenarios to ensure you know how to access and use your stockpile effectively.

### 3. Community and Networking

- **Share Knowledge**: Share stockpiling tips and resources with friends and neighbors.

- **Collaborate**: Consider collaborating with others in your community to share resources and support each other during crises.

Stockpiling essentials is a proactive step towards ensuring your preparedness for any crisis. By focusing on critical items such as food, water, medical supplies, hygiene products, and household supplies, you can create a comprehensive stockpile that supports your family's needs. Implementing effective strategies for inventory management, space optimization, budgeting, and security will help maintain your stockpile and ensure you are always prepared for emergencies. Regular maintenance and practice, along with community collaboration, will enhance your overall preparedness and resilience.

# CHAPTER 9
# KEY BUG-IN SKILLS

During emergencies, knowing how to effectively "bug in" or shelter in place is critical. Essential survival skills are necessary to ensure safety, comfort, and sustainability. This chapter focuses on the key skills you need to develop to be well-prepared for any crisis while staying at home.

## Essential Survival Skills

### 1. Water Purification

Access to clean water is vital for survival. While having a stockpile is important, knowing how to purify water can be a lifesaver if supplies run low.

### Boiling Water

- **Method**: Bring water to a rolling boil for at least one minute.

- **Effectiveness**: Kills most pathogens, including bacteria, viruses, and protozoa.

- **Considerations**: Ensure the water is filtered to remove debris before boiling.

### Using Water Filters

- **Types**: Portable filters like LifeStraw, pump filters, gravity filters.

- **Method**: Follow manufacturer instructions for each filter type.

- **Effectiveness**: Removes bacteria, protozoa, and some viruses.

## Chemical Purification

- **Types**: Water purification tablets (iodine, chlorine dioxide), bleach.

- **Method**: Add the recommended dosage to the water and wait for the specified time.

- **Effectiveness**: Kills most pathogens; follow instructions to ensure proper usage.

## Solar Disinfection (SODIS)

- **Method**: Fill clear plastic bottles with water and place them in direct sunlight for at least six hours.

- **Effectiveness**: Uses UV rays to kill bacteria and viruses.

- **Considerations**: Works best with clear, shallow bottles.

## 2. Food Preservation and Preparation

Understanding how to store and prepare food safely can extend your food supply and maintain nutrition.

## Canning and Jarring

- **Method**: Use pressure canning or water bath canning to preserve fruits, vegetables, and meats.

- **Effectiveness**: Extends shelf life and maintains nutritional value.

- **Considerations**: Requires proper equipment and knowledge of canning techniques.

## Dehydrating Food

- **Method**: Use a dehydrator or oven to remove moisture from food items.

- **Effectiveness**: Reduces weight and volume, making storage easier; long shelf life.

- **Considerations**: Store dehydrated foods in airtight containers to prevent moisture absorption.

## Pickling

- **Method**: Preserve vegetables in vinegar or brine solution.

- **Effectiveness**: Extends shelf life and adds variety to your diet.

- **Considerations**: Ensure jars are properly sealed to prevent contamination.

## Cooking Without Power

- **Tools**: Solar ovens, rocket stoves, camp stoves, and grills.

- **Method**: Use alternative cooking methods if the power goes out.

- **Considerations**: Ensure you have fuel or sunlight available and understand how to safely operate each cooking method.

## 3. Home Security and Defense

Protecting your home and family is crucial during any crisis. Knowing how to secure your home and defend it if necessary can provide peace of mind.

### Reinforcing Entry Points

- **Doors**: Install deadbolts, security bars, and reinforce door frames.

- **Windows**: Use security film, bars, or shutters to reinforce windows.

### Creating Safe Rooms

- **Location**: Choose an interior room with few windows.

- **Preparation**: Stock with food, water, first aid supplies, and communication devices.

- **Security**: Install a sturdy door with a lock.

### Self-Defense Skills

- **Training**: Take self-defense classes to learn basic techniques.

- **Tools**: Consider non-lethal options like pepper spray, stun guns, or tasers.

- **Firearms**: If you choose to have firearms, ensure you are trained and follow all safety protocols.

## 4. First Aid and Medical Care

Being able to provide basic medical care is essential during emergencies when professional help may not be immediately available.

### First Aid Training

- **Courses**: Take courses from recognized organizations like the Red Cross.

- **Skills**: Learn CPR, wound care, fracture management, and how to treat burns and infections.

### Creating a Comprehensive First Aid Kit

- **Contents**: Include bandages, antiseptics, pain relievers, medical tape, scissors, tweezers, and a CPR mask.

- **Storage**: Keep the kit in an accessible, secure location.

- **Maintenance**: Regularly check and replenish supplies as needed.

### Managing Chronic Conditions

- **Medications**: Ensure a supply of necessary prescription medications.

- **Monitoring**: Use devices like blood pressure monitors and glucose meters to manage health conditions.

- **Documentation**: Keep medical records and instructions for managing chronic conditions.

## 5. Communication and Information

Staying informed and being able to communicate with others is crucial during a crisis.

### Maintaining Communication

- **Devices**: Use cell phones, two-way radios, and satellite phones.

- **Charging**: Have backup power sources like solar chargers or power banks.

### Staying Informed

- **Emergency Radios**: Use hand-crank or battery-operated radios to receive updates.

- **News Sources**: Follow reliable news sources and local emergency broadcasts.

### Establishing a Communication Plan

- **Contacts**: Maintain a list of emergency contacts.

- **Plans**: Develop a family communication plan that includes meeting points and ways to stay in touch if separated.

## 6. Sanitation and Hygiene

Maintaining hygiene and proper sanitation is critical for preventing illness.

### Personal Hygiene

- **Supplies**: Stock up on soap, hand sanitizer, toothpaste, and feminine hygiene products.

- **Practices**: Maintain regular hygiene routines to prevent infections.

## Waste Management

- **Toilets**: Use portable toilets or create makeshift latrines.

- **Disposal**: Properly dispose of human waste to prevent contamination.

## Cleaning and Disinfection

- **Supplies**: Stock disinfectants, bleach, and cleaning supplies.

- **Practices**: Regularly clean and disinfect living areas to maintain a healthy environment.

Developing essential survival skills for bugging in is a critical component of emergency preparedness. By mastering water purification, food preservation, home security, first aid, communication, and sanitation, you can ensure your household's safety and well-being during any crisis. Regular practice and continuous learning will enhance your ability to handle emergencies effectively and provide peace of mind knowing you are well-prepared.

# Training and Preparation

Being well-prepared for emergencies involves more than just having the right supplies and skills. Continuous training and preparation are crucial to ensure that you can effectively respond to crises. This chapter will cover the importance of training, various types of preparation, and how to build a culture of readiness within your household.

## The Importance of Training

Training is essential for building confidence and competence in emergency situations. It ensures that you know how to use your survival gear, perform first aid, and respond to various scenarios effectively.

## Key Benefits of Training:

- **Skill Development**: Enhances your ability to perform necessary tasks under pressure.

- **Confidence**: Increases your confidence in handling emergencies, reducing panic and stress.

- **Readiness**: Ensures you are ready to act quickly and efficiently when needed.

## Types of Training and Preparation

## 1. First Aid and Medical Training

Basic first aid and medical training are fundamental for managing injuries and health issues during emergencies.

## First Aid Courses

- **Providers**: American Red Cross, St. John Ambulance, and local community centers.

- **Skills Covered**: CPR, wound care, fracture management, burn treatment, and how to use an AED (automated external defibrillator).

## Advanced Medical Training

- **Types**: Wilderness first aid, emergency medical responder (EMR) courses.

- **Benefits**: Provides more comprehensive skills for handling severe injuries and medical emergencies.

## Home Practice

- **Scenario Drills**: Practice responding to various medical scenarios at home.

- **Equipment Familiarity**: Ensure you know how to use all items in your first aid kit effectively.

## 2. Survival Skills Training

Developing essential survival skills is critical for ensuring your safety and well-being during a crisis.

## Water Purification

- **Training**: Learn and practice different methods such as boiling, filtering, and using chemical purifiers.

- **Scenarios**: Simulate scenarios where you must find and purify water from natural sources.

## Fire Building

- **Techniques**: Practice building fires using various methods, including matches, lighters, and ferro rods.

- **Conditions**: Train in different weather conditions to ensure you can build a fire in rain, wind, or snow.

## Shelter Building

- **Types**: Learn to construct different types of shelters, such as tarps, tents, and natural shelters.

- **Materials**: Familiarize yourself with the materials you have and practice building shelters in your yard or a local park.

## 3. Home Security Training

Ensuring your home is secure during a crisis is crucial for protecting your family and property.

### Home Security Assessment

- **Evaluation**: Conduct regular assessments of your home's security, identifying potential vulnerabilities.

- **Improvements**: Implement security measures such as reinforced doors, window locks, and security cameras.

### Self-Defense

- **Classes**: Enroll in self-defense classes to learn techniques for protecting yourself and your family.

- **Regular Practice**: Practice self-defense skills regularly to maintain proficiency.

### Safe Room Preparation

- **Design**: Create a safe room in your home, equipped with supplies, communication devices, and security measures.

- **Drills**: Conduct drills to ensure everyone knows how to quickly and safely get to the safe room.

## 4. Communication Skills

Effective communication is vital during emergencies for staying informed and connected with others.

## Communication Plan

- **Development**: Create a detailed communication plan that includes contact information, emergency numbers, and meeting points.

- **Review**: Regularly review and update the plan with your family.

## Radio Training

- **Usage**: Learn how to operate two-way radios and emergency radios.

- **Practice**: Conduct regular radio check-ins to ensure everyone knows how to use them.

## Public Speaking

- **Training**: Develop public speaking skills to effectively communicate with neighbors and community members during emergencies.

- **Scenarios**: Practice delivering important information clearly and calmly under pressure.

## 5. Emergency Drills and Simulations

Regularly conducting emergency drills and simulations helps you practice your response to various scenarios.

## Fire Drills

- **Frequency**: Conduct fire drills at least twice a year.

- **Procedure**: Practice evacuating the house, using different routes, and meeting at a designated safe spot.

## Earthquake Drills

- **Procedure**: Practice "Drop, Cover, and Hold On" techniques.

- **Evaluation**: Assess the safety of your home and secure heavy furniture and objects.

## Evacuation Drills

- **Scenarios**: Simulate different evacuation scenarios such as floods, wildfires, or chemical spills.

- **Routes**: Practice using multiple evacuation routes to ensure flexibility.

## Bug-In Drills

- **Scenarios**: Simulate scenarios where you must shelter in place, such as during a lockdown or severe weather event.

- **Procedures**: Practice securing the home, rationing supplies, and maintaining communication.

## Building a Culture of Readiness

Creating a culture of readiness within your household ensures that everyone is prepared and knows their roles during an emergency.

## Regular Training Sessions

- **Scheduling**: Set a regular schedule for training sessions, such as monthly or quarterly.

- **Involvement**: Involve all family members in training to ensure everyone is prepared.

## Open Communication

- **Discussions**: Have open discussions about emergency preparedness and encourage questions and feedback.

- **Updates**: Keep everyone informed about any changes to emergency plans or new skills to learn.

## Continuous Learning

- **Resources**: Use books, online courses, and workshops to continuously expand your knowledge and skills.

- **Networking**: Connect with local preparedness groups and attend community events to share knowledge and learn from others.

## Mental Preparedness

- **Stress Management**: Learn and practice stress management techniques to stay calm during emergencies.

- **Resilience Training**: Engage in activities that build mental and emotional resilience, such as mindfulness and meditation.

Training and preparation are fundamental components of effective emergency preparedness. By developing essential survival skills, conducting regular drills, and fostering a culture of readiness, you can ensure that you and your family are well-equipped to handle any crisis. Continuous learning and practice will enhance your ability to respond effectively, providing peace of mind and increasing your resilience in the face of emergencies.

# CHAPTER 10
# OUTSMARTING FEMA
# AND THREATS

## Understanding Threats

In the realm of emergency management, understanding threats is crucial for developing effective defensive strategies. Threats can range from natural disasters and technological failures to man-made emergencies. Each type of threat requires a specific approach to preparation and response, making it essential to grasp the nuances of each.

### 1. Natural Disasters

Natural disasters are sudden, severe events caused by natural processes of the Earth. They can cause extensive damage and disrupt communities. Understanding the characteristics and risks associated with different natural disasters helps in preparing effective defensive strategies.

- **Hurricanes**: Hurricanes are powerful tropical storms characterized by strong winds, heavy rainfall, and storm surges. They can lead to extensive flooding, wind damage, and power outages. Preparation involves several key steps:

  - **Evacuation Plans**: Develop and communicate evacuation routes and procedures. Ensure that all family members or employees are familiar with these plans.

- o **Home Fortification**: Strengthen windows and doors to withstand high winds. Install storm shutters or board up windows to prevent breakage.

- o **Emergency Supplies**: Stock up on non-perishable food, water, medications, and first aid supplies. Keep a battery-operated radio to receive weather updates.

- o **Insurance**: Review and update insurance policies to cover hurricane-related damages, including flood insurance if you live in a flood-prone area.

- **Earthquakes**: Earthquakes are sudden ground shakes caused by tectonic movements. They can lead to structural damage, injuries, and disruptions. Preparing for earthquakes involves:

- o **Structural Reinforcement**: Retrofit buildings to withstand seismic activity. Secure heavy furniture and appliances to walls to prevent tipping.

- o **Emergency Kits**: Assemble earthquake kits with essentials like water, food, flashlight, batteries, and a multi-tool.

- o **Family Plans**: Create and practice a family emergency plan. Identify safe spots within your home and establish communication methods if separated.

- **Floods**: Floods occur when water exceeds normal levels, inundating areas. They can be caused by heavy rainfall, storm surges, or dam failures. Key preparations include:

- o **Flood Barriers**: Install sandbags or flood barriers to protect your home from rising waters. Elevate electrical systems and utilities to prevent damage.

- o **Evacuation Routes**: Know your local evacuation routes and shelters. Avoid driving through flooded areas as water can hide dangerous debris and strong currents.

- o **Emergency Supplies**: Maintain an emergency kit with waterproof containers for important documents and medications.

- **Wildfires**: Wildfires are uncontrolled fires that spread rapidly, fueled by dry conditions and strong winds. Preparation for wildfires involves:

  - o **Defensible Space**: Create a defensible space around your property by clearing flammable vegetation and using fire-resistant building materials.

  - o **Emergency Alerts**: Sign up for local alerts to receive notifications about fire conditions and evacuation orders.

  - o **Evacuation Plan**: Develop a plan for quick evacuation. Include a list of important items to take and establish meeting points for family members.

- **Tornadoes**: Tornadoes are violent windstorms with rotating columns of air. They can cause extreme damage and require swift action. Preparation strategies include:

  - o **Safe Room**: Designate a safe room or storm shelter in your home. This should be an interior room on the lowest floor, away from windows.

- **Emergency Plan**: Have a plan in place for how to respond during a tornado warning. Practice tornado drills to ensure everyone knows what to do.

- **Weather Radio**: Keep a weather radio or app that provides real-time tornado warnings and updates.

## 2. Technological Failures

Technological failures can have significant impacts on daily life and business operations. As reliance on technology grows, so does the potential for disruptions. Effective strategies for managing technological failures include:

- **Power Outages**: Power outages can disrupt daily activities and critical services. To mitigate their impact:

  - **Backup Power**: Invest in generators or uninterruptible power supplies (UPS) to keep essential systems running during outages.

  - **Emergency Lighting**: Use battery-powered or solar-powered lights to maintain visibility when the power goes out.

  - **Communication Plans**: Ensure that communication methods are in place, such as battery-powered radios or alternative communication devices.

- **Cyber-attacks**: Cyber-attacks target digital systems, leading to data breaches and system disruptions. Defensive strategies include:

- ○ **Security Software**: Use comprehensive antivirus and anti-malware software to protect against malicious attacks.

- ○ **Password Management**: Implement strong, unique passwords for different accounts and change them regularly. Utilize two-factor authentication where possible.

- ○ **Employee Training**: Train employees on recognizing phishing attempts, secure handling of sensitive information, and best practices for cybersecurity.

- **Infrastructure Breakdown**: Failures in critical infrastructure, such as water supply or transportation systems, can disrupt essential services. Preparation involves:

  - ○ **Maintenance**: Regularly inspect and maintain infrastructure to prevent breakdowns. Ensure that systems are up to date with the latest technology and safety standards.

  - ○ **Contingency Plans**: Develop contingency plans for maintaining operations during infrastructure failures. This might include alternative water sources or backup transportation methods.

## 3. Man-Made Emergencies

Man-made emergencies can arise from intentional actions or accidents. These include terrorism, industrial accidents, and civil unrest. Addressing these threats involves:

- **Terrorism**: Acts of terrorism can cause widespread panic and disruption. Preparing for terrorism includes:

- **Emergency Response Plans**: Develop detailed plans for responding to various types of terrorist attacks, including bombings, active shooter situations, or biological threats.

- **Security Measures**: Implement security measures such as surveillance systems, access controls, and training for staff on recognizing suspicious behavior.

- **Public Awareness**: Stay informed about potential threats through local authorities and intelligence sources. Participate in community awareness programs and training.

- **Industrial Accidents**: Industrial accidents, such as chemical spills or explosions, can have serious consequences. Defensive strategies involve:

  - **Safety Protocols**: Adhere to strict safety protocols and regulations to prevent accidents. Conduct regular safety drills and inspections.

  - **Response Plans**: Develop and practice response plans for various types of industrial accidents. Include procedures for evacuation, containment, and communication.

  - **Incident Reporting**: Establish procedures for reporting incidents and coordinating with emergency services. Ensure that all employees are trained on these procedures.

- **Civil Unrest**: Civil unrest, including protests and riots, can pose risks to safety and property. Preparation includes:

- o **Security Planning**: Develop security plans for protecting property and personnel during periods of civil unrest. This may include increased security measures or temporary closures.

- o **Communication Channels**: Maintain open communication channels with local authorities and community leaders. Stay informed about potential unrest and respond proactively.

- o **Community Engagement**: Engage with the community to address grievances and reduce the likelihood of unrest. Support local initiatives that promote social stability and inclusivity.

# Defensive Strategies

Developing effective defensive strategies is essential for mitigating the impact of threats and ensuring a coordinated response. These strategies involve risk assessment, building resilience, leveraging technology, and fostering collaboration.

## 1. Risk Assessment and Planning

Risk assessment involves identifying potential threats and evaluating their impact on your organization or community. This process is crucial for developing effective emergency plans.

- **Conducting Risk Assessments**: Regularly assess the risks associated with different types of threats. This involves:

  - o **Historical Data**: Review historical data to understand past incidents and their impact. Analyze patterns and trends to predict future risks.

○ **Vulnerabilities**: Identify vulnerabilities within your infrastructure, systems, and processes. Consider how these vulnerabilities could be exploited by various threats.

○ **Impact Analysis**: Evaluate the potential impact of different threats on operations, safety, and resources. This helps prioritize areas for improvement.

• **Developing Emergency Plans**: Create comprehensive plans for responding to emergencies. Key elements include:

○ **Roles and Responsibilities**: Define roles and responsibilities for individuals involved in emergency response. Ensure that everyone knows their specific duties.

○ **Communication Procedures**: Establish procedures for communicating during emergencies. Include methods for internal communication and public notifications.

○ **Resource Allocation**: Identify and allocate resources needed for emergency response, including personnel, equipment, and supplies.

• **Training and Drills**: Regular training and drills are essential for ensuring that emergency plans are effective. This involves:

○ **Simulations**: Conduct simulation exercises to practice response procedures. This helps identify weaknesses in the plan and allows for improvements.

o **Feedback**: Collect feedback from participants to understand challenges and areas for improvement. Use this feedback to refine emergency plans.

o **Continuous Improvement**: Regularly update and improve emergency plans based on lessons learned from drills and real incidents.

## 2. Building Resilience

Building resilience involves strengthening systems and processes to withstand and recover from disruptions. Resilience is crucial for maintaining operations and ensuring recovery.

- **Infrastructure Improvements**: Enhance the resilience of infrastructure to withstand various threats. This includes:

  o **Retrofit Buildings**: Retrofit buildings to meet safety standards and withstand natural disasters. Use fire-resistant materials and reinforce structural elements.

  o **Redundant Systems**: Implement redundant systems for critical operations, such as backup power supplies and alternate communication channels.

  o **Regular Maintenance**: Conduct regular maintenance to ensure that infrastructure remains in good condition. Address potential weaknesses before they become critical issues.

- **Community Engagement**: Engage with the community to build collective resilience. This involves:

  o **Education and Training**: Provide education and training on emergency preparedness and response.

Offer resources and support to help individuals and organizations prepare.

○ **Collaboration**: Collaborate with community organizations, businesses, and local authorities to enhance resilience. Share information and resources to support collective preparedness.

○ **Support Networks**: Develop support networks to assist vulnerable populations during emergencies. This includes providing resources, information, and assistance to those in need.

- **Resource Management**: Ensure that resources are available and can be quickly mobilized during emergencies. Key strategies include:

  ○ **Stockpiling Supplies**: Maintain stockpiles of essential supplies, such as food, water, and medical items. Ensure that these supplies are regularly updated and rotated.

  ○ **Partnerships**: Establish partnerships with suppliers and vendors to ensure access to critical resources. Develop contingency plans for resource shortages.

  ○ **Logistics**: Plan and organize logistics for resource distribution during emergencies. Ensure that transportation and delivery systems are efficient and reliable.

## 3. Technology and Innovation

Technology plays a critical role in enhancing defensive strategies. Innovations in technology can improve early warning systems, enhance communication, and streamline response efforts.

- **Early Warning Systems**: Implement systems that provide timely alerts about potential threats. This includes:

  o **Weather Alerts**: Use weather alert systems to receive notifications about severe weather conditions. Ensure that alerts are disseminated to all relevant parties.

  o **Emergency Notification Apps**: Utilize mobile apps that provide emergency notifications and updates. Encourage community members to download and use these apps.

  o **Public Alert Systems**: Implement public alert systems that can quickly disseminate information to large populations. This includes sirens, broadcast alerts, and social media notifications.

- **Communication Technologies**: Utilize advanced communication technologies to improve emergency response. Key technologies include:

  o **Social Media**: Use social media platforms to share information and updates during emergencies. Engage with the public to provide real-time information and address concerns.

  o **Emergency Broadcast Systems**: Implement emergency broadcast systems that can reach a wide audience. Ensure that these systems are tested regularly and maintained.

  o **Alternative Communication Devices**: Use alternative communication devices, such as satellite phones or two-way radios, to maintain communication when traditional methods fail.

- **Data Analytics**: Leverage data analytics to predict and manage threats. This involves:

  o **Predictive Analytics**: Use predictive analytics to identify potential risks and trends. Analyze data from various sources to anticipate future threats and plan accordingly.

  o **Decision Support Systems**: Implement decision support systems that provide real-time data and insights for emergency response. Use these systems to make informed decisions during crises.

  o **Incident Analysis**: Analyze data from past incidents to understand patterns and improve preparedness. Use this analysis to refine emergency plans and strategies.

## 4. Collaboration and Coordination

Effective response to threats requires collaboration and coordination among various stakeholders. This includes working with government agencies, non-profit organizations, businesses, and community groups.

- **Interagency Cooperation**: Collaborate with government agencies such as FEMA to ensure coordinated response efforts. Key strategies include:

  o **Formal Partnerships**: Establish formal partnerships with government agencies to facilitate coordination. Develop agreements and protocols for joint response efforts.

- ○ **Information Sharing**: Share information and resources with government agencies to enhance response capabilities. Participate in interagency meetings and briefings.

- ○ **Joint Training**: Participate in joint training exercises with government agencies to improve coordination. Use these exercises to practice collaborative response efforts.

- **Public-Private Partnerships**: Collaborate with businesses and organizations to leverage resources and expertise. Key strategies include:

  - ○ **Resource Sharing**: Share resources and expertise with businesses and organizations. This includes providing support, equipment, and personnel during emergencies.

  - ○ **Collaborative Planning**: Work with businesses and organizations to develop collaborative emergency plans. Ensure that these plans address mutual needs and capabilities.

  - ○ **Community Support**: Engage with businesses and organizations to support community preparedness efforts. Encourage participation in community programs and initiatives.

- **Community Involvement**: Engage with community members to ensure that their needs are addressed and that they are involved in emergency preparedness efforts. Key strategies include:

o **Community Education**: Provide education and resources to help community members prepare for emergencies. Offer workshops, seminars, and informational materials.

o **Volunteer Programs**: Develop volunteer programs to support emergency response efforts. Recruit and train volunteers to assist with various aspects of preparedness and response.

o **Feedback Mechanisms**: Establish feedback mechanisms to gather input from community members. Use this feedback to improve emergency plans and address concerns.

Outsmarting FEMA and other threats involves a comprehensive approach to understanding potential risks and developing effective defensive strategies. By conducting thorough risk assessments, building resilience, leveraging technology, and fostering collaboration, individuals and organizations can better prepare for and respond to emergencies. In an increasingly complex world, proactive preparedness and strategic planning are essential for ensuring safety and minimizing the impact of threats.

# CONCLUSION

## Recap of Key Points

In this chapter, we explored the multifaceted nature of threats and the defensive strategies necessary to mitigate their impact. Here's a summary of the key points:

1. **Understanding Threats**: Recognizing and understanding the various types of threats—natural disasters, technological failures, and man-made emergencies—forms the foundation of effective preparedness. Each type of threat requires a tailored approach to risk assessment and response.

   o **Natural Disasters**: Hurricanes, earthquakes, floods, wildfires, and tornadoes each present unique challenges that necessitate specific preparation and response measures. These include fortifying homes, assembling emergency kits, and developing evacuation plans.

   o **Technological Failures**: Power outages, cyber-attacks, and infrastructure breakdowns highlight the need for backup systems, cybersecurity measures, and contingency plans.

   o **Man-Made Emergencies**: Terrorism, industrial accidents, and civil unrest require security planning, safety protocols, and community engagement.

2. **Defensive Strategies**: Effective defensive strategies encompass a range of activities aimed at reducing vulnerabilities and enhancing resilience.

   o **Risk Assessment and Planning**: Conducting thorough risk assessments and developing comprehensive emergency plans are crucial for anticipating and managing potential threats. This involves defining roles, establishing communication procedures, and maintaining resource readiness.

   o **Building Resilience**: Strengthening infrastructure, engaging with the community, and managing resources effectively contribute to building resilience. This ensures that systems can withstand and recover from disruptions.

   o **Technology and Innovation**: Utilizing advanced technologies such as early warning systems, communication tools, and data analytics can significantly enhance preparedness and response efforts.

   o **Collaboration and Coordination**: Working with government agencies, businesses, and community groups fosters a coordinated approach to emergency management. Public-private partnerships and community involvement are essential for effective response and recovery.

## Final Thoughts on Preparedness and Resilience

Preparedness and resilience are not just about reacting to emergencies but about proactively preparing to handle and recover from them. The complexity and unpredictability of threats demand a dynamic and multifaceted approach to planning and response. By understanding the nature of potential threats and implementing robust defensive strategies, individuals and organizations can better safeguard themselves and their communities.

Preparedness involves more than having an emergency kit or evacuation plan—it requires a mindset of readiness and adaptability. Resilience, on the other hand, is about building systems and communities that can endure and recover from disruptions, learning from past experiences, and continuously improving.

As threats evolve and new challenges emerge, staying informed and adaptable is crucial. Embrace technology and innovation to enhance your preparedness efforts, and foster strong relationships with key stakeholders to ensure a coordinated response. Ultimately, the goal is to create a resilient and prepared society capable of navigating the complexities of modern threats with confidence and effectiveness.

In sum, the strategies and insights discussed in this chapter provide a roadmap for outsmarting FEMA and other threats. By integrating these practices into your emergency management efforts, you can enhance your ability to respond effectively and recover swiftly, ensuring greater safety and stability in the face of adversity.

Made in the USA
Middletown, DE
03 September 2024